CHIWRITING

How to Use Endurance Training Principles to Condition Your Creative Mind, Supercharge Your Writing Life, and Finish Your Book

T.A. Pierce

Copyright © 2017 Thomas A. Pierce

ALL RIGHTS RESERVED
No part of this book may be reproduced in any form or by any electronic or mechanical means, including information storage and retrieval systems, without permission in writing from the copyright holder, except by a reviewer, who may quote brief passages in a review.

The exercise and nutritional information presented in this book are generic in nature and not intended to be a substitute for the advice of physicians and dieticians. Readers are advised to regularly consult with qualified professionals in matters related to their health, particularly with respect to any symptoms or conditions that may require diagnosis or medical treatment and before beginning any exercise or nutritional program.

ISBN 978-0-9991005-0-9

ChiWriting is the trademark of Thomas A. Pierce. All Rights Reserved.

Cover design: Greg Nehring, Clarity Design

Printed in the United States of America

For Amy

CONTENTS

INTRODUCTION 3

PART 1: THE "CHI" IN *CHIWRITING* 15

    What is Chi? 18

    The Case for Chi 20

    The Physical Matrix 29

    The Mental Matrix 34

    The Experience of Flow 40

PART 2: THE *CHIWRITING* PRINCIPLES 49

    Why Endurance Training Principles? 50

    The Three Physical Energy Systems 56

    The Three Creative Energy Systems 62

    The Three Basic Workouts 70

    The Three Basic Writing Workouts 74

    Key Planning and Training Principles 84

    Five Key Planning Principles 86

    Five Key Training Principles 106

PART 3: BECOMING A *CHIWRITER* 125

    "Minding" the Gap 128

    Three Habits of Mind 131

    Energizing: The Components of Chi 141

    Applying the *ChiWriting* Principles 162

    More Training Tips:
    Additional Strategies to Support Your Goals 186

A FINAL WORD 197

ABOUT THE AUTHOR 199

ACKNOWLEDGMENTS 201

APPENDIX 203

INTRODUCTION

If you are reading this, you are probably either a writer or want to become one. It could be that you've always wanted to write a book but never have. As far back as you can remember, perhaps, you've had a deep and natural desire to write but—for a variety of reasons—you have never taken concrete steps toward fulfilling this goal.

Maybe you've been "too busy" with work, family obligations, or any number of other commitments to devote time to your writing. Perhaps fear or anxiety about writing has held you back, or you believed you could never make a living writing so you pursued other career goals for a regular paycheck.

It could be that you have taken steps to fulfill your writing desire, but just haven't made as much progress as you'd like. Maybe you are dealing with the frustration of rejection, procrastination, writer's block, or any number of other obstacles, and you have either given up or found it very difficult to make much headway.

Possibly you've never really had a deep desire to write, but you have a great idea for a book. You want to develop your idea, write, and publish your book, but you don't really know how to make that a reality, especially with the busy life you lead.

No matter which category you fall into, or the reasons you're finding it difficult to move ahead with your writing; *ChiWriting* is for you.

I wrote it because I've been there.

How this Book Came About

Since I was a child, I've had what seemed to me a natural desire to write. I would scrawl out short stories in pencil on grade school tablet paper and mail them to *Highlights*—a children's magazine—and receive polite rejection letters in return.

In college, I took creative writing classes and even won a creative writing scholarship equal to a semester's worth of tuition—which wasn't much in those days compared to now. Still, it was validation that kept my interest in writing burning.

Then, before I graduated from college, a friend got me a job as a proofreader/copywriter. I would proofread and write short descriptions of the products featured in the catalogs my company produced. I was actually being paid to write. It seemed, at the time, to be a dream come true.

In time, I moved on to a bigger company where I wrote and produced the company's sales magazine and wrote other promotional material. I went on to work for other divisions of this company, writing marketing copy and corporate communications materials for insurance and investment products. I got raises and promotions. Later, I also freelanced for a variety of companies and also worked for an advertising agency. I was respected and appreciated by my clients and colleagues.

For a long time, earning a good living as a professional writer satisfied my desire to write. But the desire to focus on my own writing never left me. Eventually, I learned that a former professor of mine—Sena Jeter Naslund, a *New York Times* best-selling author of short stories and novels—had started a new Master of Fine Arts writing program at Spalding University in my hometown. I had always admired and respected Dr. Naslund as a teacher, a writer, and as a human being. Immediately, I wanted to attend. After so long as a corporate writer, however, I wasn't sure I had what it took. I had not written a single word outside the corporate world since college. But I knew I had to try.

Introduction

For over a year I prepared myself by reading and writing more fiction. Once I felt ready, I pulled together my application packet within a few days and submitted it. A few weeks later, they informed me that my application had been rejected.

I was crushed. I took this as evidence that I had no business trying to write and develop my own creative work, that I didn't have the ability. But I knew that many writers deal with frequent rejection, so after my initial disappointment, I decided to reapply. This time, however, I took much greater care in preparing my application packet. After a few months, I sent in my second application—and waited again. A few weeks later, a second letter arrived—I'd been accepted to the program.

The two years that followed were among the most challenging, exhilarating, intellectually stimulating, creatively productive years in my life. Over that period, I read dozens of novels, short story collections, and books on the art and craft of writing; wrote dozens of critical essays; read and critiqued the work of dozens of fellow students, and wrote a book-length collection of short stories—the form always a great love of mine—that served as my master's thesis.

Throughout my pursuit of an MFA, I maintained my full-time job in the corporate world while my wife worked 80-100 hour weeks to establish her career—on top of all this, she gave birth to our two daughters. Our oldest was born in the middle of my MFA studies, and the younger arrived just before I graduated. I also had a teenage son from a previous marriage.

Looking back, I really had no idea how I was going to successfully complete a demanding MFA program while working full-time and maintaining a household that had just grown by two babies while my wife worked an even more demanding schedule. I just plowed forward. When I finished, I was flying high with a feeling of accomplishment and the creative energy and momentum I had built up over the previous two years.

My creative writing life was well underway and my future was assured.

Or so I thought. Less than three months after graduating, on Super Bowl Sunday, all that changed.

My wife, who had arrived home earlier that day following a thirty-six-hour shift, lay upstairs sleeping as the game began. I sat down to watch the game, my infant daughter in my arms, when, shortly after kick-off, I began to experience a dull ache on the left side of my chest. I ignored it. At first, I thought I had pulled a muscle lifting one of the girls, or perhaps had a bit of indigestion from too much Super Bowl Sunday cheese dip. But before the first quarter was over, I was doubled over in pain, barely able to breathe.

I woke up my wife and she drove me to the Emergency Room. My sister-in-law took care of the kids. All the way to the hospital, I thought, what could be wrong? I was healthy, had never had any significant health problems whatsoever. It was unthinkable I could be having a heart attack.

As it turns out, I was right.

Following a chest scan, the ER doctor reported the diagnosis: multiple bilateral pulmonary emboli. Blood clots. Somehow, a blood clot had formed somewhere in my body, broke loose, and traveled through my bloodstream to my pulmonary artery where, had it been big enough, it would have killed me instantly.

Doctors administered blood-thinning medication and scanned the rest of my body for more clots—and found nothing. In fact, the doctors could find no reason that a clot had formed. Since I had no risk factors, they termed my embolism "unprovoked," and ordered extensive blood tests to find the cause.

It turns out that I have a genetic mutation called "Factor V Leiden," which basically makes the chemical chain reaction in the bloodstream necessary for blood to coagulate easier to start—even "unprovoked." Some people with Factor V Leiden

Introduction

never experience any symptoms or complications. I did. And was lucky enough to survive. But, as a precaution, I have to remain on blood thinning medication for the rest of my life.

Then, barely two months after my pulmonary embolism, I lost my job due to a company reorganization. I was out of work after twenty years in the corporate world. Suddenly, I was home during the day, caring for two young daughters while my wife continued her career.

The combination of the health scare, the loss of my job, and feeling overwhelmed with the care of two young daughters and a teenage son sent me into an emotional tailspin. The creative momentum and joy I had felt during and after completing the MFA program evaporated. I found myself drained, exhausted, and depressed.

I remember trying to bottle-feed my daughter while the other one was crying, and bawling myself I felt so depressed and overwhelmed. But I hid it well; never told anyone. I believed I had to be strong. I never seriously considered suicide, but I began to feel as if I had a better understanding of why someone might choose this drastic option.

I don't write this to elicit sympathy or to suggest that my experience was worse than what millions of others go through every day. In fact, I was lucky to be alive, lucky not to have cancer, lucky to have three healthy children and a strong marriage. But still, I was barely making it through each day. This struggle went on nearly two years.

Over that time, I wrote not a single word. Then I heard a radio ad for Team in Training, the fundraising arm for the Leukemia and Lymphoma Society. At the time, I was twenty-five pounds overweight, so the idea of getting in better shape by training for an endurance event intrigued me.

I attended an informational meeting and decided then and there to sign up for an Olympic-distance triathlon, which entails a 1500-meter swim (nearly one mile) a forty-kilometer bike ride (nearly twenty-five miles) and a ten-kilometer run (6.2 miles).

Now, understand that at this point in my life I had never swum a single lap, never run more than two miles at a time, never biked for anything but fun. I went home that day and told my wife what I had signed up for and she thought I had lost my mind—maybe I had. Nevertheless, I trained hard for the event with my Team in Training coaches and other teammates over a four-month period. Ultimately, I completed the event and raised over $5,000 for the Leukemia and Lymphoma Society.

In the process, my mental state improved dramatically; the depression lifted. I dropped the extra twenty-five pounds and felt better than ever, alive with energy. I found that I loved the discipline of exercising, the structure of following a training schedule, and the variety of the workouts. I continued to train that year and competed in other events. My new sport enamored me so much that I set myself a new goal: to complete a full-distance Ironman triathlon: a 2.4 mile open water swim, 112-mile bike, followed by a 26.2 mile run—a full marathon.

For the nine months prior to the event, I followed a six-day-a-week conditioning program comprising up to fifteen hours of training per week. (Many triathlon enthusiasts devote twenty to twenty-five hours a week for the Ironman, and elite professionals even more, but fifteen hours weekly was what I determined I could do and still meet my other obligations.) When the big day arrived, I was ready.

I completed my Ironman race in 13 hours, 57 minutes, and 22 seconds. Crossing that finish line was one of the most exhilarating feelings in my life. Afterward, I returned to Team in Training to help coach their triathlon teams so that I could help others experience the benefits and satisfaction of the sport.

Introduction

Eventually, I became a Level 1 triathlon coach, certified by USA Triathlon, and held that certification for a time.

At this point you may be asking: what does endurance training have to do with writing? Good question.

Two of my proudest accomplishments, aside from my family, are earning my MFA degree and completing an Ironman triathlon. Reflecting on these accomplishments brought me to a couple of realizations. First, they were both accomplishments that, throughout most of my life, I thought were impossible for me to achieve—yet I did. Second, they both required a tremendous amount of time and focused, disciplined effort.

Looking back, I couldn't figure out how I found the time. How, for example, was I able to complete the fifteen to twenty hours of weekly work necessary to earn an MFA degree while holding down a full-time corporate job, and taking care of two infant children and a teenager while my wife worked eighty to a hundred hours per week? The same is true of the fifteen hours I devoted weekly to endurance training for the Ironman race.

Two key insights took shape as I explored these questions. First, time-management had little to do with it. Traditional time-management techniques help you "save" time and become more efficient in your use of it. The problem with this approach is that it tends to lead to compartmentalization in which different aspects of your life are siloed, or isolated from one another.

For example, you could apply traditional time-management principles to save time at work and potentially become more efficient in performing your job responsibilities, but the time saved does not necessarily translate to your life outside of work and what you want to accomplish there—like writing a book.

Traditional time-management can play a helpful role, but it's not about finding the "time." It's about developing the *energy* (i.e., life energy or "chi"). If you have the energy, and the will, to accomplish something, it will be done, no matter the time constraints.

Developing the energy to accomplish something is primarily about choice management, not time management. First and foremost, you must make the choices that increase the available pool of life energy from which you can draw. Then it's about making the choices of where and how to focus that energy and direct it toward achieving your goals.

My second key insight was that the focused and systematic approaches I used to complete both my MFA degree and an Ironman race were remarkably similar in nature. I did not realize it at the time, but the endurance training principles that prepared me for the Ironman were the same essential principles that enabled me to complete my MFA program. In much the same way that athletes condition and develop the physical body to complete an endurance event, writers condition and develop the creative mind to complete a book (or, indeed, any other type of long-term creative project).

In other words, I realized that endurance training not only enhances one's life energy and overall wellness and productivity, it is also an effective model for planning and structuring one's creative life. Applying the principles of endurance training to your creative life can virtually guarantee that you will not only finish your book, but also improve your overall wellness and productivity in every life domain.

This book shows you how.

Part 1 explores the "chi" in *ChiWriting*. We will look at "life energy" from both scientific and spiritual perspectives to provide a philosophical foundation for an energy-management approach to achieving your writing goals.

In Part 2, we will examine the basic training and planning principles used by endurance athletes—from elite professionals to dedicated amateurs and fitness enthusiasts—and how these

Introduction

principles can be applied to your writing life to ensure creative conditioning and systematic progress toward the completion of your book.

Part 3 covers the essential strategies for implementing these training and planning principles and integrating them into your life.

Though *ChiWriting* focuses primarily on writing books, the principles can be applied to any other long-term creative goal: screenwriters, playwrights, songwriters/composers, and visual artists all can benefit from the *ChiWriting* methodology.

What this Book is Not

This book is not specifically about physical fitness or endurance training. It presents general information about physical fitness and endurance training principles, including nutrition, but it does not recommend specific fitness regimens, training plans, or diets. In other words, as a writer you *do not* have to be an endurance athlete or train for an endurance event in order to benefit from these principles.

But the book does advocate for applying such principles as a means of increasing the chi, or life energy, necessary to focus on and achieve your writing goals while maintaining key responsibilities in other areas of your life, so it is my hope that you will use the information to develop a fitness and nutritional regimen that works for you.

This book is also not specifically about the art or craft of writing. I do not cover topics intended to help you improve your writing skills, per se, such as setting, description, characterization, or how to write dialogue. Nor does this book cover other practical aspects of writing, such as publishing and marketing your work. There are plenty of wonderful books and resources out there about the art and craft of writing and how to publish and market your work.

Instead, you will learn concrete strategies and a practical approach for integrating writing into your busy life and actually completing your book. When you finish *ChiWriting*, you will be able to apply the principles of endurance training to your creative life and build a training plan for your writing (as opposed to a physical training plan) that will increase your writing fitness and condition your creative mind; a plan that will take you step-by-step across the finish line of your book (or any other long-term creative project).

Are you ready to supercharge your writing life?

Let's begin.

PART 1:
THE "CHI" IN *CHIWRITING*

"Writing a long novel is like survival training.
Physical strength is as necessary as artistic sensibility."
— Haruki Murakami

I magine three runners lined up at the start of a marathon—a foot race of 26.2 miles. The first runner is highly conditioned and has faithfully followed a proper training program for months in preparation for the race. The second is in decent shape, and leads an active lifestyle that includes a fair amount of regular, physical exercise, but has not systematically trained to prepare for the race. The third runner is completely deconditioned, out of shape, and leads a sedentary lifestyle.

Which runner is most likely to finish the race?

The answer, of course, is the first. In this scenario, it's pretty obvious that the runner who has followed a proper training program will have the highest chance of success in finishing a grueling marathon. The second runner may or may not finish, but his chances for success are significantly lower, and his chances for failure significantly greater, than they are for the highly conditioned runner. And even if she finishes, she is likely to take far longer and experience dramatically higher levels of pain and suffering in the process. The third runner has virtually no chance of finishing the race. He is likely to get no farther than a mile or two before dropping out, completely overwhelmed, worn out, and defeated by the effort. Even if he decides to walk, he is not likely to go farther than a few miles.

Writing a book is like running a marathon: crossing the finish line—that is, actually completing a manuscript—typically requires months (if not years) of systematic, focused, and disciplined effort. Yet most people who want to write a book line up at the starting line like the third runner: they're creatively deconditioned, completely unprepared to follow through, and so they may go through the motions for a while, but they are likely to drop out as soon as the going gets rough. Those like the second runner are a bit better prepared perhaps, but even if they are able to finish, it is likely to be a far more difficult process than it has to be.

If you want to write a book and are like the second or third runner, you must condition your creative mind as the endurance athlete conditions her body. The principles and strategies used by endurance athletes—both elite professionals and everyday amateurs—to train for events like marathons and triathlons are designed to promote the physiological adaptations necessary for the body to perform over long distances.

The body can't *not* adapt and improve its capacity in response to the proper training stimuli. Even if a would-be marathoner starts from a completely deconditioned physical state, if he is consistent in following a well-designed training program—one that starts slow and builds on his progress over time—his success in crossing the finish line is virtually guaranteed.

In the same way, endurance-training principles and strategies, when properly applied to the writing process, will promote the creative adaptations necessary to finish your book. Consistently following a well-designed writing program, building on your progress over time, virtually guarantees that you will complete your book or other writing project. Like the body, the creative

Part 1: The "Chi" in ChiWriting

mind can't *not* adapt and improve its capacity to perform in response to the proper training stimuli.

When I first started training for triathlons, I came across a book that eventually became the inspiration for the title of this one: *ChiRunning: A Revolutionary Approach to Effortless, Injury-Free Running*, by Danny and Katherine Dreyer. Because I had never considered myself a good runner (in fact, I hated running) I read it eagerly, looking for a way to make my training more efficient and productive—and it did, in fact, help me a great deal. The premise of the Dreyers' book is that easier, more efficient, injury-free running requires a natural flow of life energy, or chi.

And so they advise on how to set up the proper conditions for allowing such energy to flow naturally in the body when running—primarily through proper posture, form, and body alignment, but also through proper biomechanic movements, techniques, and breathing. By applying the principles discussed in *ChiRunning*, my run training became more efficient and productive (as well as more enjoyable), which in turn improved my overall triathlon preparation.

ChiRunning offers a practical approach to improving running efficiency, but its underlying focus on *chi* also fascinated me. I was familiar with the *concept* of chi as life energy, of course, but I thought of it primarily as an esoteric spiritual concept with little practical application in everyday life. The book's conceptual premise—that working with this force, this life energy, rather than against it, is the key to developing a running practice that is more effortless and enjoyable, and leads to greater overall fitness, life enjoyment, and success—really struck a chord with me.

The idea of working *with* this life force energy, rather than against it, to enhance productivity and efficiency applies not only to running, but any human endeavor—including writing books. So in this book, I have a similar objective for your writing life. *ChiWriting* is about setting up the proper conditions for developing and enhancing the life force energy, or chi, in your body and in your creative mind, allowing it to flow naturally in your life as a whole, then directing it specifically toward achieving your writing goals. How? By using the strategies and principles of physical endurance training as a model for structuring and implementing a disciplined writing program.

The goals of *ChiWriting* are, first, to enhance your awareness of chi as life-force energy and remove any existing (or potential) blocks to its free-flowing operation; then, to develop and enhance the level and flow of chi both in your life generally and in your creative life particularly; and finally, to harness and channel that chi effectively, using endurance training principles, toward supercharging your writing life — even as you continue to successfully manage all the other important responsibilities in your life, such as work and family obligations.

We start with chi.

What is Chi?

Simply put, "chi" refers to life-force energy. It is the animating force that powers our bodies and minds and all things in the world around us. The term is Chinese in origin, and can also be spelled *qui* or *ki*, but many spiritual traditions and cultures have a different name for this same basic concept. In the Hindu tradition, the life force is known as *prana*; ancient Egyptians referred to *ka* as the vital essence of life; and, in the Western Christian tradition, it is known as the *Holy Spirit,* part of the Holy Trinity, the essential force linking God the Father, the Creator of Life, to His Son, His Creation.

To be sure, "chi" is not a scientific term. Chi itself cannot be directly grasped or measured or observed, yet we can know it exists because we can observe its *effects*; there *is* an animating life force because there *is* life, both within us, as us, and outside of us, in the world we perceive and experience.

The living system of our bodies, other living creatures, and all we experience in the natural world through our senses, are physical manifestations of chi. But chi also manifests abstractly through our consciousness, our thoughts, emotions, imagination, intuition, and creativity. In fact, it is the uniquely human manifestation of chi as thought consciousness that allows us to perceive and intuit its very existence.

Chi sounds "New Agey," but of course it is an ancient concept. Since the dawn of human consciousness man has attempted to understand and explain his origin and nature and role in the universe. Chi is a way of doing that. It is easy to imagine an ancient seer or philosopher noticing that humans need not consciously breathe—it just happens naturally; or noticing that within his chest, a heart beats continuously, without any conscious effort on his part; or noticing, on a grander scale, the continual movement of the heavens and the cycle of the seasons and even the changing weather.

If all of these actions and movements and effects occur with zero conscious effort or input from man—then the question follows: what is the cause? The ancient seer, based on his observations and the lack of any scientific knowledge upon which to base any rational understanding, must have concluded that there exists a mysterious force that animates all of life and that this force must emanate from an even more mysterious Creator responsible, somehow, for creating and sustaining life in all its many forms.

As a concept, chi reflects man's natural and abiding desire to *understand* and to *know*. It is a way to make sense of the mystery of life. In that sense, it is a spiritual belief, because spiritual beliefs attempt to explain that which is essentially unexplainable—life exists, therefore there must be an ultimate Creator of life—and the basis for such belief is abiding faith in a consciousness behind all things.

But man's natural desire to understand and to know his place and role in the universe is also reflected through scientific inquiry and discovery. The scientist looks at the unexplainable and attempts to understand it by asking and answering questions that reveal logical, demonstrable facts behind the phenomena of life. What does science have to say about the concept of life-force energy? Max Planck, a quantum physicist during the late nineteenth and early twentieth centuries and a contemporary of Albert Einstein, wrote the following:

> *I regard consciousness as fundamental. I regard matter as derivative from consciousness. We cannot get behind consciousness. Everything that we talk about, everything that we regard as existing, postulates consciousness.*

Let's look at why Planck—less well-known than Einstein, perhaps, but every bit as brilliant and influential—might feel this way.

The Case for Chi

For centuries, scientists, based primarily on the work of Aristotle and Ptolemy, believed that the earth was the center of the universe and that the sun and other heavenly bodies revolved around it. In the sixteenth century, Copernicus hypothesized that the earth was not a stationary body at the center of the universe, but revolved around the sun. At the time, this was a radical and controversial idea that upended centuries of established scientific consensus. Later, however, in the seventeenth century, Galileo confirmed Copernican theory and sparked a scientific revolution.

Barely a generation later, Sir Isaac Newton built upon Galileo's work and discovered the laws of motion and the law of universal gravitation, which describe a unified theory of mechanical energy and planetary and stellar motion. Basically, Newtonian physics explain with mathematical certainty what happens in the observable world, in the relationship between the mass, force, and acceleration of an object, whether it's an apple falling from a tree or the orbit of a planet.

Part 1: The "Chi" in ChiWriting

More than two centuries after Newton's discoveries rocked the scientific understanding of the observable world, brilliant physicists like Planck, Einstein, Niels Bohr, Werner Heisenberg, and others began looking closely at what is invisible to the naked eye: the unobservable world of atomic and subatomic particles.

Through the work of quantum physicists, we know now that a rock is not just a rock, but a collection of trillions of molecules — elemental compounds that make up that particular type of rock. We know that these molecules are a collection of atoms bound together through electromagnetic and other forces in a specific configuration. We know that each of the trillions of atoms that comprise the trillions of molecules that collectively make up this rock consist of even smaller particles: protons, neutrons, and electrons, and that these subatomic particles are themselves made up of even smaller particles, such as quarks, leptons, and bosons.

And we also know that every atom is in constant motion. The electrons in each one are constantly moving at incredible speed around the protons and neutrons that form the atom's nucleus. Depending on their number, there may be different levels of electrons, creating a kind of "cloud" around the nucleus. Further, we know that the size of the subatomic particles that make up an atom are much smaller than the actual size of the atom itself, which means an atom is mostly empty space. In other words, at the subatomic level, everything, even something seemingly as solid as a rock, is mostly empty space pulsating with energy.

We actually live in a vibrating, energetic universe in which the only real difference between two seemingly discrete forms of matter is the particular patterns and configurations of the relatively few energetic particles that make them up.

This fundamental "energetic" aspect of life as we now know it was described by Albert Einstein in his 1905 paper on the Special Theory of Relativity. Up until Einstein, it was thought that time was an absolute, universal constant; that all observers in the universe, no matter their frame of reference, would experience time — a minute, an hour, a year, etc. — the same way. But the Special Theory of Relativity proved that time is relative — that observers with different frames of references would experience time differently.

For example, an observer on earth would experience time differently than an observer traveling at the speed of light. Because of this insight, Einstein conceived of time as a fourth dimension, joining the three spatial dimensions in a construct he called "space-time."

What Einstein's theory showed is that *time* is not a universal constant as previously thought; but rather, that the *speed of light* is a universal constant. This led to his famous equation, $E = MC^2$, where E = energy, M = mass (of matter) and C^2 = the speed of light, squared. This equation (validated by later experiments) revealed that energy and mass are equivalent properties of matter.

Think of a rock again: we know a rock has mass because it has weight and takes up space in three dimensions. But does it have energy? Einstein proved that it does. His equation tells us that because the collection of particles that make up the rock have mass they also have energy — and not just a small amount of energy, but a phenomenal, mind-boggling amount of energy.

If we arrive at "energy" by multiplying mass by the speed of light squared — a huge number since light travels 186,000 miles per second — then the amount of latent, or potential, energy contained within even a small amount of matter is simply staggering. Conversely, what Einstein's equation also tells us is that incredibly stupendous amounts of energy are also required to create matter.

We see both these processes at work within stars. Think of our own sun, the star that makes life possible here on Earth: like all stars, the sun is powered by a hydrogen-helium nuclear fusion reaction that has been ongoing for billions of years and will continue for billions more. This reaction continually releases an immense amount of energy in the form of heat and electromagnetic radiation (including the relatively small slice of the electromagnetic spectrum that is visible, i.e., light).

But as the nuclear reaction continues, the immense amount of energy generated also creates the particles that form the elements of matter—including two of the most important elements required for life: carbon and oxygen. To date, scientists have discovered 118 of these elements (the periodic table of the elements), each of which differs only in the number of protons and neutrons in the nucleus and the number of electrons that orbit the nucleus. (Writers of course have their own "elements"—the twenty-six letters of the alphabet from which infinite worlds can be created through the elemental compounds of words and sentences.)

If we look at all the many different forms of matter all around us, it's clear that what we see and experience in the physical world is really an incomprehensible (i.e., infinite) amount of energy organized and structured into different variations and patterns of elemental compounds, which in turn are composed of trillions and trillions of individual atoms, each of which is constantly vibrating with the movement of electrons around the nucleus.

While physical matter is made up of particles that give it mass, the particles themselves retain an immense amount of the energy from whence they came; everything we see and experience in the physical world—from our sun, to the others stars shining in the night sky, to our bodies, to the food we eat, to the ground we walk on—is made up of the same, energetic, stuff. Ultimately, what Einstein's famous equation reveals is the fundamental unity behind all of life. *Everything is connected.*

In essence, every "thing" we see and experience in the material world, including our own bodies, exists as a physical manifestation of energy within the infinitely vast field of energy from which it, somehow, came into being.

How this is possible and why it occurs is an ongoing deep mystery for which quantum physicists are still trying to develop a unified theory. But at least part of the answer may lie within the mystery of consciousness itself.

One of the strangest features of quantum physics is the wave-particle duality of matter, in which discrete particles of matter also exist as waves of energy. Early physicists disagreed about whether light energy consisted of waves or particles; but quantum physicists such as Bohr, Heisenberg, Einstein, and others, proved that light exhibited the characteristics of both waves *and* particles: light travels in waves—which are measured by wavelength, frequency, and amplitude—but it can also travel as a particle, known as a photon, or a discrete quanta of light.

After this discovery, French physicist Louis de Broglie proved that not only light, but *all* matter exhibits this same mysterious wave-particle duality; electrons, like photons of light, behave as particles but can also behave like waves. Why?

In experiment after experiment, physicists have demonstrated that matter exhibits this strange wave-particle duality, but the experiments *do not* demonstrate that this duality is some intrinsic property of either a wave or a particle; rather, whether a wave or a particle is observed depends on the observer and how the experiment is conducted. If the observer set up the experiment to measure a wave, a wave was observed; if the observer set up the experiment to measure a particle, a particle was observed. In other words, what is observed depends upon the consciousness of the observer.

This kind of quantum ambiguity is reflected and expressed in Heisenberg's famous "Uncertainty Principle," which states that both the position and momentum of a particle cannot be accurately known at the same time—if an electron's position is measured, its momentum (and therefore its future position) cannot be known, and if its momentum is measured, its present position cannot be known. So, if an electron's position is measured, its future position cannot be predicted; if its momentum is measured, its position is lost.

Part 1: The "Chi" in ChiWriting

In other words, electrons—elemental subatomic particles of matter—seem to pop into and out of existence based on the consciousness of an observer. That this is so is one of the most astounding and mysterious phenomena in quantum physics; it calls into question the nature of reality itself. Based on strange quantum behavior like this, Einstein is said to have remarked that *"Reality is merely an illusion, albeit a very persistent one."*

A concept to explain this sort of weirdness was devised in the 1920s by physicists of the day who lived and worked in Copenhagen, including Bohr and Heisenberg. Their concept, known as the Copenhagen Interpretation, basically holds that *no objective reality* exists at the quantum level, only *probabilities*.

According to the Copenhagen Interpretation, quantum particles do not exist in one particular state or another but in all possible states at once—known as "superposition." So, for example, an electron wave (like a light wave) would contain all possible states in which an electron could exist—known as its "wave function." When an observation is made, the superposition of the wave function (i.e., all of its possible states) collapses into only one of its possible states. This is known as "wave function collapse." In other words, the interaction of an observer causes all possible states to be instantaneously reduced to only a single observed state.

Of course, the Copenhagen Interpretation isn't the only theory out there. In the 1950s, Princeton physicist Hugh Everett developed an alternative theory, known as the Many Worlds theory, which has since gained some traction in the physics community. The Many Worlds theory holds that there is not a single universe in which "reality" unfolds as the superposition of a wave function collapses into a single state based on the interaction of an observer, but rather that parallel universes exist in which each of the possible states of the wave function superposition are played out.

In the 1970s, the theory of Quantum Decoherence was postulated, which basically states that wave function superpositions collapse when quantum systems interact with one another. And the Superstring theory postulates that all matter comes from constantly oscillating "strings," millions of times smaller than the smallest known sub-atomic particle, and that these strings create many other dimensions (besides the three spatial dimensions we know about) where particles that seem to pop into and out of existence "hide out."

More recently, in 2012, physicists at CERN, the European Organization for Nuclear Research, in Geneva, conducted experiments using the Large Hadron Collider, a supercollider in which streams of protons are smashed into each other at light speed, recreating the effects of the Big Bang, said to have occurred at the beginning of the universe. By doing so, they later identified a particle consistent with the Higgs-Boson particle, hypothesized to be the boson (a subatomic particle) responsible for imparting mass to other particles such as quarks and leptons (which in turn are the subatomic building blocks for electrons, protons, and neutrons) as they pass through a field of energy known as the Higgs Field.

Named after Peter Higgs, the British physicist who helped to develop the theory, the Higgs-Boson has also been referred to popularly as the "God particle" because confirmation of its existence would explain the origin of mass—how the fundamental particles that create the matter we experience in the physical world come to be.

If all of this sounds incredibly bizarre and complicated—it is. Quantum physics is an incredibly vast, mysterious, and complex field of study. I have hardly scratched the surface here and do not claim or pretend to be an expert—not even close.

So why am I even writing about these theories?

The main reason is simple: I wanted to define and establish the foundational concept of this book—chi as both spiritual and practical life-force energy—in a context that goes beyond a merely superficial, "New Agey" kind of description. All of the scientific inquiries and discoveries I've outlined here—from Copernicus to Galileo to Newton to the quantum physicists in the late nineteenth and early twentieth centuries to modern day—have been essential to our understanding of reality. But take note: despite the gigantic leaps in scientific knowledge over the history of mankind, none of it invalidates the ancient spiritual concept of chi, or life-force energy, as articulated by seers and philosophers who did not have access to the science we now take for granted.

Newtonian physics describes how and why an apple falls from a tree. Quantum physics explains the atomic and subatomic building blocks of the apple, and even how these particles interact with one another. But neither scientific worldview can explain the essential mystery behind why the apple grows and exists in the first place.

There still remains a deep essential mystery behind all of life. For example, today's scientists and medical researchers know that the heart beats because of an electrical impulse it receives from the brain; an electrical impulse that travels through neural pathways and nerves that branch out from the spinal column; they know that the heart beats to circulate oxygen-rich blood to every cell of the body, sustaining life; they can monitor the heart, measure its electrical activity and output, and diagnose and treat conditions that may be detrimental to its function—but what they don't know, ultimately, is *why* the brain generates the electrical impulse to the heart in the first place. Where does it come from, and why? The best scientists can do is call it an autonomic—or involuntary—response. It's simply there because it is.

The same applies to breathing. It's an autonomic response, for sure, but there is no ultimate scientific answer as to *why* the muscle of the diaphragm continually expands and contracts to fill and empty the lungs of air *without any conscious effort* on our parts. It simply does because it does.

Thus, the ancient seer's idea of life-force energy ("chi") remains an elegant and operative concept for thinking about life as we know it in practical terms, even though it remains rooted in mystery.

Another reason for exploring the concept of chi through a scientific lens: we will to return to some of these ideas and concepts in the more practical sections of the book. Another aspect of quantum weirdness to note here is that the effects observed at the microscopic quantum level do not apply directly to the macroscopic physical world (or rather, scientists do not yet know how they may apply). In the world we experience directly, Newtonian physics still rules. Your kitchen table does not depend upon an individual observer to exist and if you stub your toe on it in the dark of night clearly you are not stubbing your toe on an illusion.

Nevertheless the quantum concepts we've covered can be used as helpful analogies for thinking about and interacting with the world to accomplish your goals, such as:

- Time is relative. *(Theory of Relativity)*
- Everything is energy. *(E =MC²)*
- All possibilities exist simultaneously. *(Wave-Particle Duality and Superposition)*
- Results depend on conscious choice. *(Wave Function Collapse)*

I've talked about man's natural desire to know and to understand his role and place in the universe and how this desire is expressed through the work of both spiritual and scientific thinkers. To me, this suggests that, as distinct spheres of thought, spirituality and science need not be, nor should be, constantly at odds. One need not deny spirituality in pursuit of scientific knowledge, or vice versa. In fact, the opposite is true: they are intertwined and inextricable.

Part 1: The "Chi" in ChiWriting

To a remarkable extent, the advancement of scientific knowledge in quantum theory leans toward validating the concept of life-force energy. Let me return to Max Planck, one of the most brilliant and influential thinkers in the field of quantum physics, who said:

> *As a man who has devoted his whole life to the most clear headed science, to the study of matter, I can tell you as a result of my research about atoms this much: There is no matter as such. All matter originates and exists only by virtue of a force which brings the particle of an atom to vibration and holds this most minute solar system of the atom together. We must assume behind this force the existence of a conscious and intelligent Mind. This Mind is the matrix of all matter.*

The force Planck writes about is the same force ancient Chinese seers intuited as chi. It is the same force you will learn to tap into, enhance, and apply in this book to achieve your writing goals. Not only that, as a writer, your creative work is allied with both spiritual and scientific thinkers because, no matter what you write, you are searching out, exploring, and discovering the same great universal truths about human nature and the reality of the human condition.

The Physical Matrix

Wherever you are as you're reading this, bring your awareness to your body. Are you sitting, standing, lying down? Are you comfortable? How does your body feel? Do you notice tension anywhere? If so, release it. Notice your stomach. Is your stomach comfortable? Is it full from a recent meal or are you hungry? Place your hand on your chest. Feel your heart beating. Now notice your breathing. Slowly and consciously breathe in, and slowly and consciously breathe out. Then, take a deeper breath, filling your lungs to capacity, and hold for a second before breathing slowly out again.

As you breathe out, let your breath expand your awareness to your immediate surroundings. You could be alone at home, reading in bed or in a favorite chair; or you could be in a coffee shop or a bookstore, sipping coffee while you read, with other people nearby who are also sipping coffee, reading, or quietly talking. What sights, sounds, smells, and sensations do you notice? Is there a flower or a plant nearby? Notice its leaves, its stem, the soil in which it is rooted.

Now further expand your awareness to the natural environment beyond your immediate surroundings. If you are inside, perhaps there is a window nearby and you notice that a breeze outside is rustling the leaves in the trees. Perhaps it is cloudy and overcast, a gentle rain falling. Or it could be that clouds are floating by in a blue sky, the sun brilliantly shining. If you are reading at night, perhaps you can see stars shining from the window.

What you noticed, both all around you and in you, as you, is chi — the animating life force that is present in all things. Everything you noticed is moving, vibrating. Even if you can't perceive it, everything in the physical world, everything you can see, smell, hear, taste, and touch, is constantly in the process of change, exchange, and transformation — that is the presence and operation of chi in the world.

The vast majority of the time, you are not consciously aware of chi's presence and operation in the world — and even when you are conscious of it, it is still nearly impossible, through consciousness alone, to fully comprehend the stunning intricacy, complexity, and efficiency with which it operates. Your physical body is a good example.

In terms of your physical body, it is easy, for a time, to become conscious of your breathing and your heartbeat — but these are only two simple outward manifestations of the intricate work of the chi operating within you. Beneath these outward manifestations, chi is continuously powering, at every moment, all of the numerous and complex bodily systems and processes vital to maintaining life:

- Your respiratory system, in which fresh oxygen is inhaled into your lungs, and transferred to your red blood cells and the byproducts cells can't use, such as carbon dioxide, is exhaled back into the atmosphere;
- Your cardiovascular system, in which your heart circulates oxygen-rich blood throughout your body via arteries, veins, and capillaries, nourishing each cell;
- Your digestive system, in which the macronutrients (carbohydrates, proteins, and fat) and micronutrients (vitamins and minerals) in the food you eat are assimilated into the body to fuel, build, and repair cells and tissues;
- Your nervous system, which controls and regulates other bodily systems through electrical impulses that travel to and from the brain via neural pathways and nerves branching out from the spinal cord.

There are other major body systems as well, including the skeletal-muscular system, the immune system, the endocrine system, and more. In and of themselves, each bodily system is a marvel of both complexity and efficiency, but it is also astoundingly wondrous how each bodily system works together holistically, with perfect balance, harmony, and precision in the vital, intricate, and finely tuned choreography of life—each dependent on and supportive of all the others in some way. Of course, this normal operation can sometimes be disrupted by illness, injury, or disease, but when that happens, the body continues to work hard to heal and restore normal functioning; a process that is, in itself, utterly miraculous.

But the truly miraculous, ultimately mysterious, thing is that all of these complex systems operate subconsciously, that is, below or outside, your conscious level of awareness. You do not have to think about them, they simply carry out their necessary functions, going about their jobs naturally and continuously, without any effort, direction, or input from you, or even any clear knowledge about how all these complicated processes work. That is universal life force energy at work.

But chi is not limited to powering our physical bodies. Chi is the living energy that powers all of creation. We are all part of a living matrix in which chi is everywhere at all times, in which fundamental particles are constantly flowing, circulating, exchanging energies, and transforming themselves into the world of form and matter we see and experience all around us.

For our physical bodies, it starts with breath. You could, if you wanted to, consciously stop breathing for a short time, but if you did, you would soon feel the urgency of chi's need and nature to continue flowing naturally and continuously. So consider what happens when we breathe: Chi flows into the lungs from the atmosphere that surrounds us, where it is transformed into life-giving oxygen and distributed to each cell throughout the body. The oxygen is transformed into energy for the cell and the primary byproduct of that transformation, carbon dioxide, is exhaled back into the atmosphere.

Carbon dioxide, which is poisonous to humans in high concentrations, is then cleansed from the atmosphere by trees and plants through the process of photosynthesis, which uses the energy of sunlight to synthesize atmospheric carbon dioxide into the energy needed to power their growth. As a byproduct of that transformation, trees and plants then release into the atmosphere more of the oxygen humans need to survive in a continuous, reciprocating flow of circulating chi.

We see this same reciprocating flow in the food we eat. The chi of sunlight, water, and nutrients from the soil that powers the growth of fruits and vegetables is stored within them. Upon consumption, the energy stored within them is released to power our bodies. If you eat meat, you are consuming the chi stored within the animal which first came from the plants the animal ate. Even the energy we currently use to power our homes and cars and factories is derived from chi stored within ancient plant life that has, over millions of years, been transformed into fossil fuels.

The cyclic, life-sustaining reciprocity of the living matrix in which we all exist is a key characteristic of life-force energy that can be seen throughout the observable physical realm. We can see it operating in the cyclic seasons: from the rebirth and nascent life of spring, to the growth and maturation of summer, through the beautiful decline of autumn, to the desolate rest of winter.

And we can see that the seasons of earth themselves are powered by the continual movement of our planet in its defined and rhythmic orbit around the sun, itself a gigantic orb of energy that continually pulsates its life-giving heat and light to our planet. And, as it happens, the sun, ninety-three million miles away, is at the optimum distance to provide just the right amount of heat and light to power life on earth—any closer and our planet would be burned to a crisp; any farther away and it would be frozen solid.

So no matter how limited or broad our perspective—whether we focus on individual bodily processes at a cellular level or the vast movement of planets and stars in the universe or anywhere in between—we can observe the mysterious operation of chi in action, making life as we know it possible.

Simply becoming deeply aware of the presence of a life force that unifies and sustains all things in the physical reality you experience every day is the first step toward enhancing its presence in your life and harnessing it to achieve your writing goals (or any goal, for that matter). But chi is not limited to the physical realm. It is also present within consciousness, manifesting as mental energy, as thought and emotion.

The Mental Matrix

It is fairly easy to imagine and appreciate the presence and operation of chi on the concrete, physical level—we need only take the time to notice its effects on a regular basis. Yet the wondrous operation of chi in the physical world of our bodies and nature is only one of its manifestations—it also operates on a non-physical basis, at the abstract level of consciousness.

All animals have some level of consciousness, of course, but as humans we are uniquely endowed with the capacity for *self*-consciousness, for *self*-awareness, for volitional choice. Through our unique cognitive and metacognitive abilities we are able to think, emote, inquire, reflect, imagine, create, perceive, intuit, and desire. It is through these unique abilities that we are able, to a remarkable degree, to choose our experience and build our own personal realities in a way no other species can.

French philosopher Rene Descartes famously remarked, "I think, therefore I am," which is perhaps the most succinct description ever of the wonder of human consciousness. In five simple words, we can understand that consciousness is a requisite for "being" (i.e., a human *being*) in a way that aligns with quantum theory's notion that the consciousness of an observer affects physical reality.

But it also implies that, to a large extent, what each of us "thinks" about ourselves determines what comes after "I am." In other words, we, as humans, have the unique power to define ourselves according to our thoughts about ourselves. "I am" represents the wave function superposition in which all possibilities exist simultaneously, while what comes after "I am" represents wave function collapse to a single state.

Two people standing in a field may see the same fence that encircles them, but each may perceive the fence differently based on their own subjective thoughts about it—one may see it as constraining and think "I am trapped," the other may see it as protective and think "I am protected." What is the difference? Only thoughts. Different thoughts create vastly different interpretations of the same experience. How can that be so? How can it be that our thoughts, in effect, create our reality?

The answer, I believe, is that just as there exists a physical matrix that creates and sustains our objective, corporeal existence in the world of matter through the constant movement of fundamental particles, there also exists a mental matrix that creates and sustains our subjective and personal realities through the constant movement of fundamental wave energy.

Think back to the earlier discussion of wave-particle duality and superposition from the scientific perspective: Matter, or physical reality, is the result of a "wave function collapse." In the wave function, all possibilities exist simultaneously, and these possibilities somehow "collapse" into a single state through the observation and intention of an observer. Somehow, observation and intention (in quantum experiments, at least) cause wave energy to transform into particle energy, to create the "stuff" we experience in the physical world.

But there is a problem here: remember that this kind of quantum weirdness doesn't translate to the physical world where Newtonian physics still rules. Again, a kitchen table does not depend on the intention of an observer for its existence, and though an individual human mind may be capable of affecting an experiment at the quantum level, certainly it cannot possibly sustain that affect at a macro, physical level. So how is it that matter in the macro world, in all its myriad forms, exists at all?

Let's return to the Max Planck quote I referred to earlier. Planck, who devoted his entire life to science and the study of matter, said that all of his research indicated that "there is no matter as such." He said that "all matter originates and exists only by virtue of force which brings the particle of an atom to vibration" and holds it together, and that behind this force is "a conscious and intelligent Mind," which is "the matrix of all matter."

Science cannot prove absolutely, of course, the existence of this conscious and intelligent Mind—science only led Planck to postulate its existence. Here, we butt up against the limits of science to where faith must take over. So how might we have faith in a conscious and intelligent Mind behind all things?

Imagine that this conscious and intelligent Mind conducted an experiment very much like quantum physicists did when they discovered wave-particle duality and wave function collapse. Imagine that this Mind intended to measure particles where only wave energy existed before and that through this thought, through this intention, the world of matter was created. From a universal perspective, then, we can say that the entire universe, the whole of creation exists as a result of the thought and intention of this conscious and intelligent Mind.

From a single thought of this conscious and intelligent Mind, a universal wave function superposition—featuring an infinite array of possibilities—collapsed into the world we sense and experience, a world that has unfolded over billions of years and will continue to unfold for billions more. Because of our limited perspective, it is impossible for the human mind to fully conceive of the "infiniteness" of a Mind that could create the universe and everything in it—but if we think in terms of the linear time we understand, it isn't difficult to imagine that the hundreds of billions of years that the universe has been *and will be* in existence is equivalent to only a fleeting thought within this infinite Mind.

It could be that the universe and everything in it, including you, me, and everyone else, exists as a single instant of thought within this infinite Mind—a thought that both created the physical and mental matrices through which we experience our world and is playing out through them.

Recall that the physical matrix that sustains us depends on a reciprocal flow and transformation of life force energy—from planetary and stellar motion to the changing seasons to the food that fuels our bodies to the vital exchange of oxygen and carbon dioxide between humans and plants. There is also a reciprocal flow and transformation of thought energy sustaining the mental matrix that creates our personal realities, our unique experience of the world.

Your life can be thought of as a wave function with a superposition of possibilities available to you, an infinite number of possibilities that already exist within the conscious and intelligent Mind that Planck called "the matrix of all matter." It is your own thoughts, your own choices, your own actions that collapse the superposition of the wave into your personal experience.

From a spiritual perspective, well-known author Deepak Chopra writes about a "field of pure potentiality in which there exists an infinite array of possibilities waiting to manifest as experiential, dimensional, physical reality." This concept is essentially analogous to the scientific theory of wave function superposition. According to Chopra (and other spiritual thinkers), the causative agent that creates that manifestation from pure potential (in which everything already exists) is our own thoughts, emotions, and actions. To me, the parallel here between spiritual and scientific thought is striking.

Think about what both of these worldviews imply: they imply that anything you (or any other human being) could ever imagine is not only possible, but already exists somewhere within a field of energy. It already exists—otherwise, it could not be imagined. The Wright Brothers were able to bring flying machines into existence because that possibility already existed within this energetic matrix. Edison was able to bring the electric light into existence because that possibility already existed within this energetic matrix. They intuited these possibilities, imagined them, and then took action to manifest their visions.

This applies also to the book you want to write.

Think of it like this: your book already exists within a mysterious field of energetic potential; it already exists, because *all* possibilities exist simultaneously within the realm of energetic superposition. In order to manifest your book, actually bring it into existence from energetic to physical form, you must collapse its superposition through the focused application of chi in both its forms: thought energy (imagination) and physical energy (the action of putting words on the page).

Chi is the channeling link between infinite potentiality and manifest reality. But note that chi in both its forms—thought energy and physical energy—are required.

Imagine floating in a boat on the vast ocean; in the distance, stretched across the far horizon, are an infinite number of ports, each one representing some different future life experience. You can float and drift and not take any focused action or thought and you will eventually drift into one of the ports—which one? No one can say. You could end up anywhere.

And what happens if you just start paddling, without any real mental focus on where you end up? You will end up in one of the ports, but probably not the one where you really want to be. Upon arrival, you may look around the port and ask, "How did I end up here?" Conversely, what happens if you keep your eyes on a single port—you are mentally focused on the port you want—but you don't do any paddling? Despite your mental focus, you won't get very far.

In either scenario, you are, in effect, drifting, because in either one, you are not likely to end up where you really want to be. You could choose your port, mentally focus on it, and start actively paddling toward it, but what happens if you lose your mental focus, if you start thinking about one of those other ports? You're going to end up way off-course.

Conversely, you could start out with absolute mental clarity about where you are going, and paddle toward your destination, but then lose the physical energy necessary to paddle—then what happens? Mentally, you are still focused on the port you want to reach, but without physical energy and action you are not going to make progress; you end up, again, drifting, not likely to reach your desired destination.

So the link between physical energy and action and mental energy and focus—chi in its different manifestations—is vital to achieving any goal, including writing a book. Writing is thought of as primarily a creative and mental task, with very little physicality involved; however, if you do not take physical action to put words on the page, you are simply drifting toward nowhere. There is always, in any creative endeavor, a fundamental link between thought (mental energy) and action (physical energy).

When thoughts do not match actions or actions do not match thoughts, there is dissonance, less power, scattered energy that produces less effect. And of course if there is no action at all, despite great thought or imagination, nothing is produced. You may have the desire to write (thought energy) but until your desire to write lives in action, it cannot come into being, into reality.

Action is the absolute requirement. The alignment of thought and action is where the mysterious alchemy of manifestation occurs. There is energy in desire, but without action, it has nowhere to go. Action opens up the pathway for the energy to flow through and become manifest in your experience.

Imagine your book or writing project, your thoughts, ideas, and desire for it. You've had these thoughts, ideas, and desire for a while, but haven't acted upon them, for whatever reason. Because you have not acted on them, or not acted on them in a focused and systematic way, they are still within in this field of pure potentiality —what Jung called the collective unconscious, and Planck called the energetic matrix of all matter.

And there they remain, available to be accessed by others who have similar thoughts, ideas, and desires. (How many times have you had an idea, but not acted upon it, only to see that someone else had the same idea but acted to make it a reality?)

It is the mechanical action of actually sitting down, opening your notebook or turning on your computer, taking a pen in hand or putting your fingers on the keyboard, and physically creating — letter by letter, word by word, sentence by sentence, paragraph by paragraph, page by page — that opens the channel for that energy to flow in, that releases it from the field of formless potential and makes it manifest in the world of form.

The Experience of Flow

When physical energy (action) and mental energy (thought and imagination) are in alignment and working together, not against each other, the magic of creation and manifestation will happen. Aligning thought and action takes discipline and focus. Discipline and focus seem difficult and effortful, but they are not. It's much more difficult and effortful to try and accomplish something when you are undisciplined, unfocused, and easily distracted.

Einstein demonstrated that the concept of time is relative, that the experience of time depends on your frame of reference. You have no doubt experienced this phenomenon for yourself. When you are involved in an activity in which you are not fully engaged or focused, the activity becomes frustrating, and you are easily distracted, little progress is made, while time drags slowly on.

But when you are fully focused on an activity, you become aware only of what you are involved in and doing at that present moment. Distractions melt away, and in that present moment of awareness, time loses meaning, and so it seems to cease to exist — time flies away. Two hours of focused effort may seem like two minutes once you look up from your work. This is when you make the most progress, when you are most efficient, when your efforts seem effortless. This is the experience of *flow*.

Part 1: The "Chi" in ChiWriting

In his books *Flow* and *Finding Flow*, author and positive psychology expert Mihaly Csikszentmihalyi (pronounced Me-high Cheek-sent-me-high) explores the phenomenon of this experience. According to Csikzsentmihalyi, "flow" is a mental state of complete and single-minded immersion in a task or activity. This state is characterized by feelings of positive energy, enthusiasm, and great satisfaction, even joy or rapture, while performing the task.

The experience of flow can happen during any type of activity — work, play, hobbies, exercise. When you feel it, you are "in the zone," a space of total but effortless concentration in which optimum performance occurs, in which your mental and physical states are completely aligned and focused.

For an endurance athlete, the flow experience is often characterized as a "runner's high." For the writer, it is an experience in which the words seem to flow effortlessly onto the page, almost as if the writer is simply taking dictation from a higher consciousness, when the "muse" visits. This is when the characters in a story are often said to "take over" as if they themselves, not the writer, are dictating and controlling the story. In such a state of flow, the writing process is energizing, exhilarating, and the writing product is often quite good.

What does it take to achieve a flow state in any endeavor? Csikzsentmihalyi writes that one must achieve an "autotelic" personality. He explains:

> *"Autotelic" is a word composed of two Greek roots:* auto *(self) and* telos *(goal). An autotelic activity is one we do for its own sake because to experience it is the main goal. For instance, if I played a game of chess primarily to enjoy the game, that game would be an autotelic experience for me; whereas if I played for money, or to achieve a competitive ranking in the chess world, the same game would be primarily exotelic, that is, motivated by an outside goal. Applied to personality, autotelic denotes an*

individual who generally does things for their own sake, rather than in order to achieve some later external goal.

To be a writer, it seems to me, one must derive autotelic satisfaction from writing. If one wants to write or has a desire to write a book but hasn't, one can say that an autotelic personality for writing has not yet been developed. Look at this from the perspective of many of the excuses you have probably used to not write, even though you want to (I have certainly used them):

- Lack of time/too busy
- Fear of failure
- Procrastination
- "Writer's block"
- Feelings of inadequacy (not being good enough/smart enough/talented enough)

If we were able to really hone in on what was stopping you or tripping you up, we could come up with a strategy to fix it. For example, if you really lacked the time to devote to your writing project, there are lots of time-management techniques and organizational strategies we could employ to give you more time to write. Would that do the trick?

Or perhaps you identified fear of failure as your ultimate roadblock, or feelings of not being good enough or smart enough. We could spend some time really analyzing the source of your fear and inadequate feelings and work to eliminate them. Would that work?

For every reason you, or anyone else, came up with for not writing, we could devise a workable strategy to resolve it or circumvent it. But, again, would it matter? If you are really honest

Part 1: The "Chi" in ChiWriting

with yourself, the answer is likely no. If you found more time due to increasing your efficiency, you would not necessarily spend that time writing. If you were able to eliminate your fear of failure and feelings of inadequacy, that would not necessarily pull you to the page.

So what then, is the real problem? The real problem can be summed up like this: writing is not yet an autotelic experience for you. If it were, you would do it, regardless of the excuses for not doing it listed above.

If writing were an autotelic experience for you, lack of time and procrastination would not be issues, for you would seek out the pleasure and satisfaction of writing for its own sake. Similarly, fear of failure and feelings of inadequacy would not be issues because the act of writing itself would produce pleasure and satisfaction enough, irrespective of any potential future outcomes, such as advances, publication, royalties, awards, acclaim, book sales, etcetera.

The truth is, any reason (or excuse) you can come up with for not writing is secondary to the primary lack of autotelic satisfaction. If you have the desire to write, but don't, you simply do not derive enough intrinsic satisfaction from the writing process itself in order to make it worthwhile for you.

For you, the struggles of writing outweigh the pleasures of writing. And so to protect yourself from the struggles of writing, you have constructed these thoughts—*I don't have time, I'm afraid of failure, I'm not smart enough*—that have caused you to choose not to write. From the field of pure potentiality, in which infinite possibilities exist simultaneously, these thoughts have collapsed the wave function superposition into the reality you are currently experiencing—a reality in which your book doesn't exist. Yet.

You can try to change these thoughts using mental energy alone. You can begin thinking and saying to yourself, *I can make the time, I'm not afraid of failure, I am good enough and smart enough.*

In fact, this is what numerous popular books about positive thinking and the so-called "law of attraction" advocate: All you need to do to change your life is change your thinking; all you need to do to manifest what you want is to think about what you want.

But this is a limited truth.

Simply changing your thoughts often fails for two reasons: one, the new thoughts don't feel true to you deep down, so they don't stick and you return to old patterns of thinking; and, two, as we talked about above, even if the new thoughts do stick, they will not necessarily lead you to take the actions required. Remember that both thought (mental energy) *and* action (physical energy) are required to manifest the experiences we say we want.

Recall the boat in the middle of the ocean with a horizon in the distance that represents an infinite array of possibilities. We can set our sights on the port we want and focus all of our mental energy on that port; we can even think to ourselves, *I have the ability to paddle there*, but unless we actively paddle toward that port and sustain that physical energy until we arrive, we are still just drifting.

So if changing our thoughts alone doesn't necessarily lead to a corresponding change in action, what can we do? We can reverse that equation. Instead of relying on new thoughts to lead us to take new actions, we can take new actions that will lead us to new thoughts.

As discussed above, the reason you are not currently accomplishing everything you want to accomplish with your writing is not just the limiting thoughts you keep telling yourself; the real reason is that you don't find writing an autotelic experience for you and so avoid it. But you can change that, and you can change it by taking action. Through proper training, you can condition your creative mind to become accustomed to the writing process and, as a result, you can actually transform the writing process into an autotelic experience.

Part 1: The "Chi" in ChiWriting

As writing becomes autotelic, your thoughts naturally change to support it. As your thoughts change to support the action of writing, your thoughts and actions become more congruent and aligned. As your thoughts and actions become more congruent and aligned, your power and momentum increases, progress flows, and manifestation follows. No longer will you think you have no time to write, you will just naturally integrate writing sessions into your life. No longer will you think you're not good enough or smart enough, you will have demonstrated to yourself that you are, in fact, good enough and smart enough. You will create that which you once thought was impossible to create.

Let me give you an example of what I mean based on my own experiences in the Ironman triathlon. At one point in my life, completing an Ironman race was literally impossible for me. My thoughts about the Ironman were: *I do not have the physical or mental ability to endure such an event, I am overweight and out of shape, I do not enjoy working out, I do not have time to work out.*

Simply changing my thoughts about the sorry condition of my body and my lack of time would not have led to a corresponding change in action. Action had to come first. So as hard as it was, I started exercising, I started to follow a training plan. In the beginning, my thoughts weren't always congruent with my actions, but I persisted. Little by little, as my body adapted to the training and as my physical condition improved, so did my thinking.

Little by little, my thoughts and actions became more congruent and aligned. Time was less of a limiting factor; my workouts somehow became integrated into my life. I began to believe I did have the physical and mental ability to complete an Ironman. And, perhaps most importantly, training became an autotelic experience for me. I came to enjoy working out simply for the sake of working out, for the positive feelings it gave me, irrespective of my goal of crossing an Ironman finish line. Many times during long runs or bike rides, I felt the "flow" Csikszentmihayli writes about.

I believe the creative mind can be trained and conditioned for optimum performance just as the body can. That is why the structure, planning, principles, and protocols involved in endurance training provide an excellent model for creative training.

In the next section, we discuss these endurance training principles and how they can be applied to the writing life, but before we move on, one last thought: You have probably heard this well-known paraphrase of a longer quote by Henry David Thoreau:

Go confidently in the direction of your dreams.

That's great advice if you're confident. Confidence is a mental state of great power and energy. But what if you're not confident? What if you are starting not from a place of confidence in your abilities but a place of impossibility—of feeling like whatever it is you want to accomplish, such as writing a book, is far beyond your reach?

You don't let a lack of confidence stop you in your tracks. You take action. You take one small step, then another, and another. What you will find is that you will pick up confidence along the way. So I have a corollary to Thoreau's famous dictum:

Go confidently in the direction of your dreams – and if you can't go confidently, go anyway.

PART 2:
THE *CHIWRITING* PRINCIPLES

"Mere literary talent is common; what is rare is endurance, the continuing desire to work hard at writing."
– Donald Hall

You have probably heard it said that writing a book—whether it's a novel, memoir or nonfiction—is like running a marathon. This is more than an apt analogy. The premise of *ChiWriting* is that you can use endurance training as a practical model for organizing and powering your writing life. You can utilize the same principles, strategies, and techniques athletes use to condition their bodies for completing endurance events to condition your creative mind, supercharge your writing life, and complete your book.

There is not a serious endurance athlete anywhere, no matter how talented, who does not use a consistent, focused, disciplined, and progressive approach to preparing for races using some combination of the training principles I will share with you. Similarly, no matter how much natural writing talent you may possess, you will not be successful unless you employ a consistent, focused, disciplined, and progressive approach to getting words on the page. That's what *ChiWriting* is designed to do for you.

In this section, we will discuss the parallels between physical and creative energy systems, then focus on the basic physical workouts endurance athletes use and how these same concepts can be applied to creative writing "workouts." We'll also look at the most important training and planning principles endurance athletes use and how these principles can be can be mapped to the "endurance event" of writing a book. But first:

Why Endurance Training Principles?

Why do endurance-training principles for athletes offer a good training model for creativity? Both concepts are geared toward the achievement of a long-term goal. Both require focused, disciplined, consistent effort. Both require consistent use of mental and physical resources. Both offer a pathway to devising a highly individualized program and outcome based on relatively few principles common to all participants.

And both programs can be scaled to suit each individual's objective. If, for example, you are an aspiring Olympic athlete working to qualify for the USA team every four years, you are going to follow a very different training regimen than an amateur athlete who wants to go from the couch to completing her first 5K run. Yet each utilize similar techniques and strategies over different time frames to achieve their goals.

Similarly, someone who wants to write a long historical novel with multiple characters and complex plotlines is going to follow a different regimen than someone who wants to write a short children's book. Yet both will use essentially the same tools, techniques, and strategies to accomplish their goals. And both must oftentimes be accomplished while maintaining focus on the other aspects of one's life that require consistent attention, including family responsibilities and work obligations.

After I achieved two long-term goals—earning an MFA degree and completing an Ironman triathlon—I asked myself how I was able to accomplish these goals while still meeting demanding responsibilities in other areas of my life. Without even realizing it,

Part 2: The ChiWriting Principles

I used similar strategies for both—the same strategies I am going to show you in this section. But there is another key ingredient that was necessary for me and will be necessary for you: commitment. All the strategies and principles in the world will not be enough to ensure success unless you have the commitment to apply them consistently over time. But *commitment* is a scary word for most people.

Author and peak performance strategist Tony Robbins says that most people "dabble." What he means is that most people fail to achieve their goals because they lack commitment. They have the real desire to do something, and they may start; they may "dabble" in it, but without commitment, it is all too easy to give up and revert to old habits. Every new year, for example, millions of people resolve to get in better shape. Gyms across the country are filled to capacity in January, maybe February, but by March, the gym crowds start thinning as people drop out, give up on their goals, and revert to the sedentary lifestyle they're more comfortable with. They had the desire to get in shape, but they only dabbled in it, their commitment to the goal waned and finally disappeared.

As a writer, or someone who wants to write a book, you may have had a similar experience. You have the desire and you start out strong, but over time—usually a relatively short time—the commitment weakens and wanes until there is not enough left to power you forward day after day. Why? What happens?

A couple of ideas to consider here: first, commitment is not a one-and-done decision, it's a *daily* decision. There is a single moment of choice when you first make a commitment—when the wave function collapses—but that point of commitment must be renewed every day. This sounds like hard work, and it is, and that's why for many people it wanes over time.

That is why you need a plan.

A good plan takes a long-term goal like writing a book or running a marathon and breaks it down step by step so that you know every day what you need to do to accomplish that goal in the end. When you have a plan like that, the only thing you need to do on any particular day is what your plan calls for. That's it. If you focus on whatever your plan calls for on any given day, rather than looking too far into the future, it is much easier to renew your commitment every day and track your progress.

If you can do that day by day, eventually you will find that you have created a new habit. But not just a habit. Importantly, you will find that you have created for yourself an *autotelic* experience. You will find that your daily engagement in these activities is its own reward; you derive internal satisfaction from engaging in these activities, irrespective of any external rewards they may or may not bring you.

At that point, you will find that the necessity to maintain commitment wanes but in a different, much more positive way. Your commitment to these activities wanes because it seems much less like hard work—and even if it does still seem hard at times, the inner rewards make it more than worth the effort, and it is these inner rewards you seek. Once you reach this stage, you may find yourself entering more and more into the flow state that tends to accompany autotelic experiences, a state in which effort seems effortless, even joyous.

So there is that moment of choice, a moment of truth, in which you actually commit to doing what it takes over time to achieve your goal. Then, to sustain that commitment over time, it is best to develop a plan and follow it through day by day. *ChiWriting* will give you the tools, strategies, and principles to develop and follow through on your plan. But the commitment to begin—not the desire to begin, but the commitment—that moment of truth, is up to you.

Are you there yet? Are you ready to commit?

If not, here is the second idea I want you to consider: One thing that keeps many people from making the commitment necessary to achieve any long-term goal is the belief that they need to *do* something before they can *be* something. Like many people, you may believe that you only *become* something after that something — whatever it is — has been accomplished.

You may believe, for example, that you are only an endurance athlete *after* you have crossed the finish line of an endurance event. Similarly, you may believe you are only a writer *after* you have written and published a book. That kind of thinking is a mistake that keeps you firmly stuck in place, unable to move forward despite desire. It necessarily causes you to be future-focused rather than fully present in the moment. It causes you to believe that who you are is dependent on something that hasn't happened yet, which only reinforces that you aren't who you want to be.

That mental stance can bleed the focus and energy required to maintain commitment to actually reach a goal. Your goal of writing a book, or whatever else it is that you want to do or be or have, may seem so far away, so difficult to reach, that you say, "What's the use?" It becomes easy to revert to old thinking and old habits that keep you where you are instead of where you want to be. It creates the illusion that what is possible for you is limited by your present circumstances. On a purely energetic level, this illusion causes the wave function superposition — in which all possibilities are available to you — to collapse into the experience of *not* doing or being or having what you say you want.

True commitment transforms that limiting belief. True commitment separates those who desire and those who actually achieve their desires. The moment you truly commit yourself to becoming an endurance athlete, for example, you *are* an endurance athlete. On a purely energetic level, the moment you make a true commitment, the wave function superposition collapses and you become an endurance athlete. In the beginning, you are simply a deconditioned athlete who has begun the necessary process of conditioning your body to complete the goal.

Similarly, the moment you commit yourself to becoming a book author, you *are* a book author. In the beginning, you are simply a deconditioned author who has begun the necessary process of conditioning your creative mind to complete the goal.

Remember that anything that happens or exists in the physical world of form first existed in the energetic realm of pure potential. Only awareness of that potential (the idea) and commitment to the thought *and* action necessary to manifest it can bring it into being, into experience. Committing to a goal is the moment of choice that collapses the wave function superposition. Then it becomes a matter of integrating into your daily life the necessary consistent thought and action (i.e., mental and physical energy, or chi) aligned with your commitment.

This is an important point: By "integrating" into your daily life consistent thought and action aligned with your commitment, I don't mean merely rearranging your schedule or moving responsibilities and tasks around in an effort to "make" more time which you may then devote to your goal. I mean cultivating the chi — or energy — that powers your life and everything in it, managing that energy and directing it toward the achievement of your writing goals through a plan of action, thus creating the conditions for your success.

Recall that chi — life-force energy — is everywhere at all times. Everything in the physical world, everything we experience, is unified at an energetic level. Everything, in fact, *is* energy, just in different forms and configurations that exist only as part of a greater matrix or field of energy. We, as individual beings, are not truly separate from this energetic matrix but integrated into it.

Most people use time as the primary organizing principle for their lives. They schedule time, make time, spend time, and save time. In a life already crowded with responsibilities, the achievement of a personal goal is often deferred until there's "more time." While managing time effectively is certainly necessary and valuable, the problem is that there never is "more time." We all have the same number of hours available to us every day and though we may be able to free up some time through efficient time management, we are never able to increase the amount of time available to us; no matter how efficient we are, constant demands arise to swallow up our time.

What can we do?

Rather than using the external structure of time as the primary organizing principle for our lives, we can use the internal system of chi.

Chi is a wonderful concept to use as an organizing principle for your life as a writer — which is to say your life itself, since there really is no desirable reason to separate the two. We cannot increase the amount of time available to us, but we can increase the flow of chi in our lives. We can create the mental and physical energy necessary to achieve our goals, and with that energy, we can naturally make the best investment of our time. As energy flows more smoothly, so does the time we have. We become far more productive than we would be using time-management techniques alone. Creating the conditions for success as a writer, then, involves primarily energy management, not merely time management.

What I am asking you to do — with suggestions of how — is to approach your writing life in the same way an endurance athlete approaches a marathon, or an Ironman triathlon, or a century bike ride. The endurance athlete enhances her life energy through focused and disciplined training principles that condition her body to complete an event. As a *ChiWriter*, you will enhance your life energy using those same principles to condition your creative mind.

You do not have to become an endurance athlete in order to put the principles they use into practice as a writer — but you would do well to put them into practice at some level that suits you as a way to increase the levels of physical and mental energy available to fuel your writing efforts. Since everything is connected at an energetic level, you will find that as your physical energy increases, so will your mental energy and, in turn, your creative energy.

But first I want to give you some background on a couple of other related endurance training concepts that can be of help in fully understanding and applying these principles: the three energy systems of the body and perceived level of exertion.

The Three Physical Energy Systems

Energy is produced and utilized by the body using three different metabolic pathways—ATP-CP, Anaerobic, and Aerobic—depending on the amount of energy required and how long it is required (i.e., the intensity and length of the physical effort).

ATP-CP

ATP-CP is the "start-up" energy system of the body. "ATP" stands for a chemical compound called Adenosine Triphosphate. "CP" stands for a chemical compound called Creatine Phosphate. When muscles need immediate energy, for, say, getting up off the couch to grab a snack or lacing up your shoes for a run, ATP in the cells is broken down to provide that energy.

When ATP is broken down to provide energy, Adenosine Diphosphate (ADP) is the byproduct. Creatine Phosphate is then utilized by the cell to resynthesize the ADP back into ATP where it is again broken down to ADP and resynthesized again to ATP, and so on.

This is an immediate and short-term energy source for the body. ATP breakdown provides energy for just a few seconds, while the cyclical process of resynthesizing ADP into ATP using CP provides energy for about thirty seconds before the other energy systems are recruited.

Anaerobic

The anaerobic energy system produces energy for intense levels of activity. The term "anaerobic" means "without oxygen," meaning that it produces energy without the use of oxygen. (The ATP-CP system is also anaerobic because it does not utilize oxygen to produce energy.) Once ATP stores in the cells are exhausted, the anaerobic system produces energy primarily by breaking down glycogen (glucose) stored in the muscles and liver, along with some fat (fatty acids stored as triglycerides in the muscles and fat cells of the body).

Glycogen breakdown produces lactate (lactic acid), which quickly builds up in the muscles and bloodstream. When the lactate threshold (sometimes called the anaerobic threshold) is reached (i.e., the point at which lactate builds up in the muscles faster than it can be removed by the body) the muscles fatigue. It is lactic acid build up that causes the burning sensation in the muscles during intense activity.

Depending on the level of conditioning, the anaerobic energy system can power highly intense activity (at or near maximum effort) for up to a few minutes before the muscles fail — muscle failure is due to the inability of the body to continue producing energy anaerobically because of lactate build-up. At that point, you are forced to stop or reduce the intensity of the activity to lower levels so that lactate can be removed from the muscles.

Aerobic

The aerobic energy system produces energy for sustained light to moderate levels of activity. The term "aerobic" means "with oxygen," meaning oxygen in the bloodstream is used to help produce energy by breaking down glycogen in the muscles and liver, and triglycerides in the muscles and fat cells. Compared to the anaerobic energy system, aerobic energy production burns a higher percentage of fat stores and a lower percentage of glycogen stores; therefore, the amount of lactate produced in muscles as a byproduct of glycogen breakdown is lower and can be removed by the body before it builds up to fatigue-producing levels.

For this reason, aerobic energy production can continue for long periods—up to two or three hours, again depending on conditioning level—before glycogen stores in the muscles are exhausted and glucose needs to be replenished. For endurance events lasting over three hours, this is why it is important to take in some form of nutrition (in addition to hydration), such as sports drinks or gels containing sucrose and fructose, which are forms of sugar that can be quickly and easily assimilated and used as glucose by the body.

The body uses a combination of these energy production systems at varying times depending on the intensity, duration, and type of activity. After "start-up" stores of ATP-CP energy are depleted, the anaerobic and aerobic systems kick-in. The higher the intensity level, the more the anaerobic system is used and the faster lactate builds up in the muscles until the lactate threshold is surpassed—at which point, the muscles fatigue quickly. The goal of physical conditioning for endurance events is to push the lactate threshold higher; a higher lactate threshold enables the body to move farther, faster, over a longer period of time at aerobic energy levels.

Rate of Perceived Exertion

Before we move on to discuss how these energy systems apply to endurance training and by extension to writing (creative training), it will be helpful to look at another concept: Rate of Perceived Exertion, or RPE, for short. RPE is simply a subjective self-assessment of how hard your body is working in any given circumstance. This is important because it is helpful to know which energy system is primarily being utilized during training.

For athletes like sprinters, training the anaerobic energy system is most important because this is the system used during

Part 2: The ChiWriting Principles

short, intense bursts of activity. But for endurance athletes, training both the anaerobic and aerobic systems is most important, since a blend of these systems is used for both speed and sustained levels of effort over long periods; therefore, knowing which system is primarily being utilized during training is important.

Many athletes rely on knowing their maximum heart rate and calculating "heart rate training zones" to determine when and how to manipulate utilization of the desired energy system during training. For example, a thirty-year-old male athlete with a maximum heart rate of 190 beats per minute might stay within a ninety to 100 percent heart rate zone (or 170 to 190 beats per minute) for short, intense periods to train the anaerobic system. To train the aerobic system, he might stay within a fifty-five to sixty-five percent heart rate zone (or 105 to 125 beats per minute).

There are many good resources online with information about how to calculate your individualized maximum heart rate and training zones. If you prefer to use the heart rate training zone method, I encourage you to seek out this information, particularly if you do actually want to participate in endurance events; however, there is a simpler method you can use for basic training to improve your overall fitness and energy levels. For purposes of this book, I am going to use this simpler RPE method.

As the name implies, when using the RPE method, you simply rate your perceived level of exertion according to a predetermined scale. Some RPE scales feature ten levels of exertion and others feature twenty levels. For the purposes of this book, I am going to keep it very simple and use a scale of one to five:

- Level 1 RPE: Light activity, warm-up.
- Level 2 RPE: Easy, comfortable pace; able to maintain a conversation.
- Level 3 RPE: Moderate pace; able to talk sporadically.

- Level 4 RPE: Hard pace, just below lactate (anaerobic) threshold.
- Level 5 RPE: All-out, maximum effort, at or above (anaerobic) lactate threshold.

To train the aerobic energy system, you would work primarily at RPE levels 2 and 3. To train the anaerobic energy system, you would primarily work out at RPE levels 4 and 5. Training both systems is important for the endurance athlete. You'll see later in this section how all this translates to your writing and creative training, but for now, let's look at why training both energy systems is important to the endurance athlete.

Imagine how these energy systems and the RPE scale would be applied to a highly deconditioned person, someone who leads a sedentary lifestyle and gets no physical exercise — the proverbial "couch potato." Such a highly deconditioned person might reach lactate threshold just walking around the block: physically speaking, heavy breathing starts, and the leg muscles burn and fatigue easily.

By the time he reaches the end of the block, maybe sooner, he's done; he must rest and recover before moving on. It's important to note here, that there is nothing "wrong" with the body in this state; the body is simply highly adaptive and, in this case, it has adapted to a lack of activity. Little demand has been placed upon the muscles and aerobic system; therefore, muscle strength and aerobic capacity have not developed. The lactate threshold is low and easily reached, and when the lactate threshold is reached the body simply cannot sustain much more physical activity; the muscles will fail.

Lactate threshold is a physical limiting factor. But there is also a mental limiting factor at work. As that highly deconditioned person walks, as the leg muscles work to propel the body forward, as the body's energy systems are recruited to provide the necessary energy, the mind also goes to work. The mind, detecting that the body is moving beyond its "normal" level of physical activity, starts alerting him to stop. About halfway around the block, mentally, he will want to give up. The mind tells him to stop. He may say to himself, "This is too hard" or "I can't go on" or "I need to rest." This is because, like the body, the mind also is not accustomed to that level of activity. To the mind, something out of the ordinary is going on so its natural reaction is to stop it.

This is the mental limiting factor, just as low lactate threshold is a physical limiting factor.

This mental limiting factor usually kicks in *before* the muscles fail due to lactate build up. Why? Because the mind is trying to protect the body. The body and mind naturally try to work together, so when both are accustomed to inactivity, both consider that the norm and tend to work together to maintain that stasis. When the body approaches lactate threshold, there is a certain amount of physical discomfort involved, and the mind will engage to try to stop the discomfort and avoid possible injury.

In order to get "in shape" then, two things must happen in concert. Physically, the lactate threshold must be pushed higher; mentally, the mind telling the body to stop must, at least initially, be ignored. The body must be trained to endure higher levels and durations of activity and remove lactic acid from the muscles during that activity more efficiently—that leads to the ability to move farther, faster, and for longer periods.

In order to move the lactate threshold higher, however, a certain amount of suffering must be endured. That also means the mind must, to an extent, be ignored during this process. If the mind detects that the body is suffering, it will scream at you to stop because it wants to protect the body. Sometimes, maybe often, the mind kicks in to prevent you from even starting! "What's the use?" it might say; or "It will take too long to get in shape," or " It's too much trouble," and so you remain on the couch.

Now look at what would happen if this same deconditioned person walked around the block every day for a number of weeks. Both the mind and the body would, fairly quickly, adapt to this new level of activity. The mind, sensing that this level of activity is the new "norm," would stop objecting; and the body, too, would respond and adapt to this new level of activity. The lactate threshold would be pushed slightly higher so that, during the walk around the block, the aerobic energy system would primarily be utilized, as opposed to the anaerobic system, which had been utilized more at the beginning when the lactate threshold was lower.

This is, in essence, the process necessary to become more physically and mentally well-conditioned: pushing the lactate threshold up through increased levels of activity and then, when the mind and body have adapted, increasing the level of activity again—either through increased time/distance covered (e.g., walking more than one block) or through increased intensity (e.g., jogging around the block rather than walking) to stimulate further conditioning gains.

The Three Creative Energy Systems

Now, let's explore how this physical system—the three energy pathways that power your life—can apply to your creative writing life.

The mind adapts to its level of creative activity in much the same way the body adapts to its level of physical activity. If you do not use it very much, the creative mind will become deconditioned and of limited functionality beyond the basic thought that you'd like to be a writer, or the basic idea you might have for a book—a plot, or a character, and so on—much like the deconditioned coach potato has limited physical ability beyond the basic necessity to move off the couch now and then.

To move beyond the basic, habitual norm, you must condition the creative mind in the same way the body is conditioned—

through progressive, sustained, focused, and disciplined effort. For the writer, there are three "creative energy systems" at work that are roughly akin to the physical energy systems:

1. Ideas: As the ATP energy system is to the body, idea generation is to the creative mind. Ideas are the "start-up" fuel.

2. Imagination: As the anaerobic system is to the body, imagination is to the creative mind. Imagination goes all-out.

3. Revision/editing: As the aerobic system is to the body, revision and editing are to creative mind. Revision/editing go slower and are more deliberate.

Ideas

Physically, when you get up off the couch and walk to the kitchen for a snack you're using energy (i.e., marginally more energy than you use at rest), but in a limited and short-term way that will not lead to overall conditioning or to the achievement of a goal like completing an endurance event. A deconditioned couch potato may have the thought that he should get in shape through a program of exercise, but the prospect seems so difficult, so far away, that the thought is dismissed and he goes back to the comfort of the couch, snack in hand.

Similarly, in merely having a creative thought or idea, you are using creative energy (or at least marginally more creative energy than you are using with a random thought), but in a limited, short-term way that will not lead to overall creative conditioning or to the achievement of a goal such as writing a book.

A deconditioned writer may have the thought that she would like to write a book, or have an idea for the book, or a great title or a character or a line of dialogue may come to her, but the prospect of developing these ideas—or not knowing *how* to develop them—and taking them to fruition seems so difficult, so remote, that the thought is quickly dismissed. And so the idea, as good as it may have been, goes nowhere and eventually withers and dies.

In the case of the couch potato, the deconditioned body is able to move in limited functional ways, but to move beyond that requires the recruitment of the other two energy systems in a focused and disciplined effort to force the body beyond its comfort zone, stretch its limitations, and force it to adapt. It is as the body adapts to new stimuli that gains in fitness and physical ability are made.

Having ideas about completing an endurance event and wanting to get in shape is fine, but it takes more than just walking between the couch and the fridge to get it accomplished. You must take specific, progressive actions to condition your body properly. You must get up off the couch and walk not to the fridge but around the block, then a mile, eventually running a mile, then more, again and again.

In the case of the would-be writer, the deconditioned creative mind is able to generate ideas and desire but to move beyond that stage requires the recruitment of analogous creative energy systems. You may have good ideas for a book and want to write it, but it's going to take more than good ideas to get it done. You must condition your creative mind by taking specific, progressive actions that force your creative mind to move beyond its comfort zone, stretch its limitations, and force it to adapt.

It is as the creative mind adapts to new stimuli that gains in writing and creative ability are made. You must get your ideas on paper and then develop them by writing a paragraph, then a page, then more, again and again. You do that by recruiting the two other creative energy systems: imagination and revision/editing.

Part 2: The ChiWriting Principles

Imagination

Use of imagination in training the creative mind is analogous to use of the anaerobic energy system in training the physical body. In the same way that pushing your anaerobic threshold higher through intense effort conditions the body to perform more efficiently overall, pushing your creative threshold higher through intense imaginative effort conditions the creative mind to perform more efficiently overall.

The mistake an aspiring writer tends to make is that he assumes his imagination is — or should be — already fully developed and conditioned; and so when his imagination at first fails to adequately expand or develop a creative idea, he just assumes he can't do it. He becomes discouraged and stops. That's like the deconditioned couch potato who gets winded walking around the block and then just assumes that her body is not capable of completing a marathon. She gets discouraged and stops. But of course, she *is* capable of completing a marathon — it just takes the proper conditioning through training and discipline.

Recall that the anaerobic system produces energy without oxygen. Because the body cannot function for long without oxygen, the anaerobic energy system is used only for relatively short, intense, powerful bursts of physical exertion. It's at or near all-out effort, an RPE of Level 4 or 5 (with the scale we're using). You are breathing heavily, and because you are pushing up against your physical limit you are probably experiencing physical discomfort. Physical discomfort engages the mind. When the mind recognizes that your body is experiencing a level of exertion beyond the norm, it will start feeding you thoughts of stopping. As soon as you approach that threshold, your mind will want you to stop and will tell you to stop: "This is too hard!" "You can't do this!" "What's the use?" "Just stop!"

Remember that the point at which you are pushing beyond your comfort zone, when the mind engages to tell you to stop, is the point when conditioning begins, and growth happens. Yet it's also when the mind seems like an enemy, like it's fighting against you. Most people will either give in to the mind's urgings and give up, or they will fight with their minds and tell themselves to stop having those thoughts or else simply try to ignore them.

Obviously, listening to the mind and stopping will not result in any conditioning. Fighting or ignoring these thoughts and pushing on a little further will result in conditioning, but at the cost of greater mental struggle. But there's a better way.

When the mind seems to be fighting your physical efforts, you tend to view it as the enemy, but it's not. It's only trying to protect your body. So instead of fighting it, instead of telling yourself not to have those thoughts, which only sets up more mental struggle, you acknowledge those thoughts, you tell your mind "thank you" for looking out for your body, that you know it's only trying to help, but that you've got your body under control. This will help to quiet your mind—the thoughts that tell you to stop or that you can't do it—and enable you to push on a little bit further.

Again, it's important to push on just a little further, just a little longer, because that is where the physical conditioning happens. By first quieting the mind—the thoughts that tell you to stop—you remove that mental limiting factor so that conditioning can happen, so that the body becomes accustomed to higher levels of physical exertion.

When that happens, the mind is eventually quieted altogether. After a few weeks of regular physical exertion, the mind will no longer interfere. Because you've effectively moved your physical lactate threshold up, you are capable of more intense effort at a Level 5 RPE than you were when you started, and the limiting factor of your mind will not kick in until you begin to approach the new higher levels of exertion.

Part 2: The ChiWriting Principles

Whereas before, in a deconditioned physical state, the mind may have engaged and begun telling you to stop at, say, an RPE of 3, now, in a more conditioned state, the mind recognizes that that level of exertion is fine and natural. Continuing to push beyond that new comfort zone will result in an even higher threshold until you reach the point where the mind and the body are seeming to work together harmoniously in the effort; where the aerobic system can hum along at much higher pace than before, so that you can perform at that level for long periods. You may even have transformed that level of physical activity into an autotelic experience — one you enjoy for its own sake, irrespective of the benefits it offers — which positions you to more easily enter a flow state.

Virtually the same process occurs when you condition your creative mind. If you are a deconditioned writer, you have probably had the thought many times that you should write a book, that you will write a book someday — just as a deconditioned athlete has the thought that she will get in shape someday. And what has stopped you? The same things that stop anyone from getting in shape — lack of time, lack of a plan, lack of motivation, etcetera.

So what needs to happen?

Like the deconditioned athlete, the deconditioned writer simply must start to move beyond her creative comfort zone. Let's say you do that by sitting down to write a page. As a deconditioned writer, that one page may be extremely difficult to complete — like a deconditioned athlete who reaches his anaerobic threshold walking around the block, you may hit your creative threshold quickly.

In the beginning, your creative threshold will be low. Creative exertion beyond the norm, beyond what your creative mind is accustomed to, will provoke limiting thoughts in much the same way that physical exertion beyond your body's norm provokes limiting thoughts telling you to stop or give up. In this case, these limiting thoughts (let's call them your internal editor) might tell you things like, "What do you think you're doing?" "This will never amount to anything." "Your writing sucks. This is crap." Or "Give up now!"

All writers have this internal editor—it's necessary and ultimately beneficial in later stages of the writing process. But in the beginning it can be nasty. It will attempt to dissuade and discourage you—and it often succeeds. For this reason, writers tend to view the internal editor as an enemy, but it's not. It is serving a purpose.

Just as the mind engages and tells you to stop during physical exertion to protect you, your internal editor does the same thing and for the same purpose: to protect you. It doesn't want you to fail. So instead of treating your internal editor as an enemy and fighting it, instead of telling yourself not to have those kinds of thoughts, which only sets up more internal conflict, you acknowledge those thoughts, you thank your internal editor for looking out for your best interests, that you know it's only trying to help, but you've got this under control. Then you push on a little bit further, because pushing *beyond your comfort zone* is where creative conditioning—like physical conditioning—happens.

By removing the limiting factor of your internal editor too early in the creative conditioning process, the imagination becomes accustomed to higher levels of creative exertion, and the negativity of the internal editor eventually quiets altogether. After a few weeks of regular creative exertion, your internal editor will interfere less often.

You've effectively moved your creative threshold up; you are capable of more intense effort than you were when you started. No longer a limiting factor, your critical internal editor will come into play only when you are ready to invite it in—not at the beginning, but later, when editing and rewriting are more beneficial.

The internal editor comes to recognize this new level of creative exertion is fine and natural, thus it won't attempt to torpedo the creative process with its withering negativity. Eventually, you may even transform your creative efforts into an autotelic experience — an experience enjoyed for its own sake, irrespective of the ambitions attached to the larger project — and again, this positions you to more easily enter a flow state, a zone of creative energy in which the writing streams smoothly forth, unimpeded.

Revision/editing

Another pathway for creative energy is a slow, careful writing process that appropriately engages your internal editor, not in an overly negative or critical way, but in a way that supports and enables editing and rewriting to polish, refine, and improve. Once the creative threshold is raised as described above it becomes much easier to engage in this process. The creative energy of a deliberate, careful revision and editing process is analogous to the body's aerobic energy system.

When the body's anaerobic threshold is raised and the body becomes more aerobically conditioned, you feel like you could run all day. You run at a comfortable pace that you could sustain for a long time, and you feel good doing it; your mind and your body are working together harmoniously to move you along with what seems like little effort. Endorphins are released leading to a "runner's high," you're in the zone, running joyously, with great energy.

When you apply this "aerobic" conditioning concept to your writing life, you experience a similar level of harmony. Your internal editor, which at the outset seemed like your enemy, has quieted its haranguing and is instead working with your creative mind. You are able to engage in the revision and editing process at a good pace over a period of time in a harmonious way with what seems like relatively little effort, at least compared to the effort it took in the beginning.

This is the product of having conditioned your creative mind using regular writing "workouts" just as the athlete uses regular physical workouts to condition the body to work harder with less effort. When demands are placed upon the body, the body responds and adapts. It can't *not* respond and adapt. It quite naturally becomes capable of much more than you ever thought it capable of. The same is true of the creative mind: when demands are placed upon your imagination, your creative mind responds; it stretches, it grows, it adapts. It becomes conditioned to perform more efficiently. It becomes capable of much more than you ever dreamed possible.

Endurance athletes train their physical energy systems to condition the body using three basic types of workouts, applied by utilizing specific training and planning principles that ensure consistent progress. *ChiWriting* is meant to train your creative energy systems in much the same way. You will apply these same training and planning principles to your writing life, and it all starts with three basic workouts.

The Three Basic Workouts

Every endurance athlete is different and every endurance athlete trains differently, but they all use the same basic workouts and the same fundamental training principles. These are the techniques and the strategies that anyone can use — not just elite athletes — to make progressive improvements in physical conditioning and optimizing the physical training process and athletic output. As you will see, you can apply these same techniques and strategies to your writing life to make progressive improvements in conditioning your creative mind and optimizing your creative process and output.

I am going to go into a bit more detail on the endurance training and conditioning principles and workouts than you probably need in order to adapt these concepts to your writing program; however, I am doing so because it will help you to develop the regular exercise program I wrote about in Part 1, which will help enhance your overall energy levels — energy you can put to productive use in your writing and other areas of your life.

There are three basic types of workouts utilized by endurance athletes — and anyone else who wants to improve overall energy and physical fitness levels:

- High Intensity Interval Training (HIIT): these workouts are shorter in duration (ten to thirty minutes) and feature repeated cycles of short intervals (up to sixty seconds) of near-maximum to maximum effort (RPE of Level 4 to 5) followed by an equal or longer period of active recovery — that is, continuing to move, rather than just stop, at an easy pace (RPE Level 2).

- Tempo Training (TT): these workouts are usually up to forty to sixty minutes and feature longer intervals (five-, ten-, fifteen-minutes, etc.) of medium to hard intensity efforts (RPE Level 3 or 4), followed by periods of active recovery at an easy pace.

- Long, Slow Distance Training (LSDT): these workouts are longer in duration (typically at least sixty minutes or more) at a steady, easy to moderate pace (RPE Level 2 or 3).

All three workout types are important because they all train different aspects of the body's energy system.

High Intensity Interval Training

Plenty of research suggests that high intensity interval training (short bursts of maximal efforts with periods of active recovery in between) is a very effective way of increasing both speed and endurance. The key to successful interval training is that the intervals must be all-out maximum efforts — by the end of the timed interval, your body should be screaming to stop. These are generally shorter workouts, but by the end of the workout, you should be tired from the intervals.

By continually pushing the limits of your anaerobic (or lactate) threshold, your body becomes accustomed to hard effort. Interval workouts will increase your anaerobic threshold (the point at which the body begins to metabolize energy without oxygen) so that, over time, you can swim, run, or bike at a faster pace aerobically (with oxygen).

An aerobic pace, in turn, enables you to work out for longer periods. Your endurance is improved; you are better conditioned. Where before, when deconditioned, walking a mile at a twenty-minute pace might seem very difficult and you'd be spent afterward, you could now run that same mile in ten minutes — and be able to continue on.

Tempo Training

Tempo workouts — in which you dial in longer periods of sustained "comfortably hard" efforts (just below anaerobic threshold): five-, ten-, fifteen-minutes, etcetera (again with active recovery periods at a slower pace between efforts) — are also great for endurance training, as they train the body to sustain a faster pace over time.

It's another way of pushing the anaerobic threshold higher, but you hold it there for a longer period than a short all-out interval. During these longer tempo intervals, a comfortably hard effort would feel like you could keep going for awhile, but at the same time, you'd be happy to slow down or stop. These longer periods of efforts just below anaerobic threshold also help build mental endurance.

Long, Slow Distance Training

The third type of workout is a long effort at a slower pace to build endurance. Even with the benefits of high intensity interval and tempo training, endurance events require longer endurance training. Longer efforts are also great for getting athletes mentally adapted to the long, sustained effort required during multi-hour endurance events.

Don't worry about speed during these workouts; just keep your effort at a comfortable, steady pace. Here, we're talking about a Level 2 or 3 RPE where you are not pushing your body to produce energy anaerobically, but keeping at a fairly easy aerobic pace; there is a balance between effort and the ability to continue that effort over a longer period.

A good endurance training plan encompasses all three of these types of workouts. How you structure each workout and how you combine workouts into an overall training regimen depends on your goals. If your goal is to get in shape, feel better, and have more energy, you could reach that goal by just doing HIIT. But if your goal is to complete a marathon, then you would do well to incorporate the other two training methods because you train both physically and mentally in different ways that are essential to completing a multi-hour event.

By combining all three workout types, you should see your endurance pace increase over time and be fully prepared to successfully cross the finish line.

The Plateau Effect

Mixing up all three types of workouts will also help you avoid the plateau effect—the point at which your body has adapted to a certain level of activity and therefore conditioning gains stop. Let's say you are deconditioned and decide to start walking around the block. At first, it's difficult. But your body quickly adapts to this new level of activity and the walk becomes easier.

Yet if you stay at that same level of activity, if you just continue walking around the block, no further conditioning gains will be made because you are no longer pushing the body beyond its prior limit. Your conditioning has "plateaued" or flattened out. If you continue walking around the block, you will maintain that level of conditioning but you will not gain anymore.

The great thing about high intensity intervals is that they are self-adjusting: no matter how fit you are, as long as you push yourself to the limit of your capability, they push your body past its current conditioning level so that further improvement is possible—and they accomplish this without a long workout, so they are time-efficient. (To avoid injury, be sure to warm up completely before attempting intervals—and don't stop to recover; keep moving at an easy pace to recover.)

What has all this to do with writing?

As you will see, these concepts can be applied to the writing life to progressively improve *creative* conditioning so that you can successfully write and complete your book. In the next section, I talk about the planning and training principles you can use to structure an effective writing regimen using these three basic workouts. But first, let me give you an idea of how applying these same workout concepts to your writing life will train your creative mind and allow you to make consistent progress on your book.

The Three Basic Writing Workouts

ChiWriting is about applying the principles of endurance training to your writing life so that your creative mind is conditioned to efficiently complete the "marathon" of writing a book just as the athlete conditions her body to efficiently complete an actual marathon or triathlon. Therefore, as a *ChiWriter*, you will "train" using three basic writing workouts that are similar in nature to the workouts endurance athletes use as discussed above:

- **High Intensity Writing (HIW):** consistent with its physical counterpart, the HIW workout is short and intense. You simply write as quickly as you can without stopping for at least fifteen minutes. You don't edit, you don't worry about spelling or grammar or punctuation or sentence structure, you just get as much down as possible in fifteen or twenty minutes. For this workout, you can use a notebook and pen (or pencil) or your computer keyboard — whatever works best for you. I like to use a notebook and pen because the words flow better for me that way.

- **Tempo Writing (TW):** this writing workout, like its physical counterpart, requires a slightly longer effort, perhaps thirty to forty-five minutes. It blends intervals of fast writing with brief periods of review, revision, and expansion that begin to shape the writing overall. Here, you begin keyboarding what you wrote down quickly on paper during the HIW workout. You type quickly, transcribing your HIW work; you still don't worry much about spelling, grammar, or punctuation at this point, but if a better word or phrase comes to you while transcribing the HIW work, you type it in; if another idea or line of thought occurs to you, go with it, typing it down quickly before it's gone. In this way, you not only keyboard and transcribe your HIW workout, you expand upon it.

- **Long, Slow Distance Writing (LSDW):** also similar to its physical counterpart, this writing workout is characterized by a slower pace that is sustained over a longer period, typically at least an hour, but you could go as long as you are able, two or three hours, or longer depending on your schedule. Here, you take the raw material that you have gathered from your HIW and TW training sessions and shape it, work with it at a slower place; trim where it needs trimming, expand where it needs expansion; correct where it needs correcting; sharpen where it needs sharpening. Here you pay attention to structure, to word choice, to language, to syntax. Here is where you hone and polish your writing.

These workouts can be combined and structured in myriad ways to build a highly individualized regimen that addresses your particular situation and produces incremental improvements over time that ensure the ultimate achievement of your goal—but the key is to incorporate all three types into your writing regimen.

Focusing just on HIW efforts will enable you to fill up notebooks fairly quickly, but that won't result in a finished book. Similarly, focusing just on LSDW may eventually result in a complete manuscript but it will likely take you much longer than it needs to and involve much more pain and struggle. The goal of combining all three writing workout types is to condition the creative mind so that you can complete your book efficiently and with a positive degree of struggle.

All three workout types are important because they each train different aspects of your creative energy system, as discussed earlier. These three creative workouts are the foundation of an effective writing regimen that progressively conditions your creative mind, just as the three physical workouts they are based on serve as the foundation for an effective physical training regimen that progressively conditions the body. Remember, faced with inputs that force the body to move beyond its comfort zone, the body *will* adapt and improve. It cannot *not* adapt.

The same is true of your creative mind.

Why is High Intensity Writing important? The goal of HIW is to stretch your creative mind beyond its current limits, so that it becomes accustomed to creative output; this will quiet that internal editor that tends to make itself loudly known way before it's actually helpful, and not in a friendly way. Have you ever sat down to a blank page to write and your internal editor immediately starts haranguing and criticizing your efforts? It can stop you in your tracks, sometimes even before a single word is written.

Recall that the mind also does the same thing to the deconditioned athlete who wants to get in shape. As soon as the mind detects a level of activity beyond the norm, its starts feeding the athlete-in-training demanding thoughts to stop; however, if the athlete does stop when the mind tells him to, no conditioning will take place. There will not be enough activity for the body to adapt to. The athlete must ignore those demands and push the body to its limits, again and again, until adaptation occurs, until conditioning happens, until the body's limits are expanded. At that point, the mind that before attempted to stop the athlete in his tracks will quiet down and begin to trust the body. That is what high intensity interval training will do for the athlete.

The same thing happens to the writer-in-training. As soon as the internal editor detects a level of creative activity beyond the norm, it sets about feeding the writer negative thoughts that thwart the process. The internal editor can be really nasty, telling the writer how bad the writing is, that the writer sucks, that she is just wasting time and effort; or, it can force the writer to rework a paragraph, a sentence, a phrase, a thought over and over again so that at the end of the writing session, not much was accomplished.

Either way, progress halts. No creative conditioning takes place. The writer must ignore negative feedback from the internal editor and push the creative mind to past its limits, again and again, until adaptation occurs, until creative conditioning occurs, until the creative mind's limits are expanded. At that point, the internal editor that before attempted to stop the writer in her tracks will quiet down and begin to trust the creative mind. That is what high intensity writing will do for the author.

The goal of Tempo Writing is to extend the ability to write over longer periods while the internal editor is quieted. During the HIW, you will push the limits of your creative mind, stretch it out a bit, over a short period, without the burden of worrying about the finer aspects of writing. During the TW workout, you step back a little; you still write quickly without too much concern over the granular aspects of editing and revision, but you begin to shape and expand the HIW writing effort.

Recall that the goal of physical tempo training is to sustain a comfortably hard effort over a longer period; you aren't pushing your body to the max but you also are not taking it easy. This has the effect of pushing your anaerobic threshold higher, so that your body becomes much more efficient at metabolizing energy and removing lactate (the byproduct of energy production) from the muscles. This, in turn, enables you to run farther and faster at a normal pace, without physical failure from lactate build-up and, importantly, without interference from the mind telling you to stop. Once the body is conditioned, the mind comes on board; it starts working with you, not against you.

Creatively speaking, the TW workout will have a similar goal. You aren't writing as quickly as you can (as in a HIW workout) in order to shut down the internal editor, but neither are you working slowly, editing as you go. At a TW workout pace, the creative mind is intensely engaged but focused more on developing and expanding the writing because the pace is slightly slower.

Here, you are shaping the raw material produced in the HIW workout, and may even add more raw material as the creative mind feeds it to you, building upon it, without undue influence from your internal editor, which remains in the background. Don't bother with considerations like sentence structure, word choice, spelling or grammar—all that comes later, during the Long, Slow Distance Writing workout. This has the effect of pushing your creative threshold higher, so that your mind becomes much more efficient at metabolizing creative energy and removing the influence of the haranguing internal editor that can stop you in your tracks.

Part 2: The ChiWriting Principles

The goal of LSDW is to engage the creative mind fully but at a less intense (more "aerobic") pace, one that's sustainable over a longer period so that you can write more swiftly and engage the internal editor when necessary, but in a more harmonious way. Instead of haranguing you, the internal editor becomes helpful. Instead of criticizing and urging you to stop, the internal editor, having become accustomed to regular creative output, works with you, not against you.

Here is where you correct, edit, trim, revise, restructure, reword as you go. Here is where you change sentence structure or move paragraphs around to improve the narrative flow. Here is where you refine and polish where you can. But, still, don't worry too much about getting the writing to a point where you feel it's completely finished—that will come later, when the complete manuscript is done.

Mixing up all these writing workouts also avoids the plateau effect in creative conditioning—just as a physical conditioning plateau is avoided through the use of all three physical workouts. Over time you will discover that your HIW workouts are much more productive than they were when you first started. The same will be true of the other two writing workouts. You will get much more accomplished in TW workouts; you will be much more efficient and productive during your LSDW workouts.

Whereas before, for the deconditioned athlete, walking a slow twenty-minute mile required an RPE of Level 3 or 4, that same RPE, once the athlete is better conditioned, results in running much faster and further—two miles or more in that same twenty minutes. Whereas before, for the deconditioned writer, writing a single paragraph in an hour's time required a creative RPE of Level 3 or 4, that same creative RPE, for the well-conditioned writer, now yields two pages of raw material in a quarter of the time. That is the power of *ChiWriting*.

In the next section, I'll have more to say about how to actually use these workouts to build an individualized writing program, but for now, let's look at a short example of where these basic workouts are able to take you.

Combining the Workouts

One HIW session of fifteen minutes (handwritten on paper) might yield two pages of raw material, depending on how fast you write. Let's say you have a character in mind, or a narrative situation, or a setting. You describe the character or situation or setting. Begin there and write as quickly as you can about whatever comes to mind. Keep the pen moving an don't stop for fifteen minutes, never pausing to edit or correct yourself, never worrying about grammar or punctuation.

If your internal editor starts mouthing off, you might thank it for its concern as you pass it by and just continue writing. It doesn't matter if what you are writing will ultimately be changed or even cut; in fact, it probably will be changed or cut. It doesn't matter because the goal of HIW is not finished material. The goal of HIW is creative conditioning—eliminating undue influence from the critical internal editor and generating raw material. You're just taking a blank page and quickly making it less blank. Fifteen minutes and you're done. Goal achieved.

For the TW workout, you invest thirty to forty-five minutes during which you keyboard the raw handwritten material generated in the HIW session. You work fairly quickly, not stopping to overthink matters of word choice or sentence structure or spelling or grammar; here do expand where you can; if you see a thread of an interesting thought from the raw material, pick up on it, keep going with it, quickly, to get it down.

If you find yourself keyboarding material you think is no good, that's okay, make a leap of faith and just keep going. Don't allow your internal editor to take over yet. At the end of the TW workout, you might have turned two pages of handwritten material into two pages of typescript, which means over the course of two writing workouts totaling about an hour, you've generated perhaps 500-600 words. Not bad.

Now, do that three or four more times over the course of a week and potentially you have around 2,000 words or more to work with — about eight to ten typescript pages, double-spaced — all in about four to five hours of "workout" time. Are they finished words? Are they polished words? Likely not. But what you have is a nice chunk of material to work with, to shape, and to polish. That's where the next workout, the LSDW session, comes in.

With the LSDW session — let's say it's a two-hour workout at the end of your writing week, maybe a Saturday or a Sunday — you are taking the eight to ten pages of raw material and working with it for a longer period at a slower pace. Here is where you invite your internal editor to help. Over time, if you've trained well, your internal editor no longer acts as your enemy at the beginning of the creative process. Now, your internal editor trusts you more, and you trust it more. It is working with you, not against you.

Over the course of a two-hour LSDW, you and your internal editor begin to shape the material. You pay attention to structure and syntax and word choice; you correct where necessary, you punctuate where necessary. If you see an incomplete thought, complete it, or if your internal editor decides it doesn't belong, strike it. But remember, the goal is not perfection, the goal is simply to work with what you have and make it better. At the end of your LSDW session, you still do not have to have a final version of those pages. That comes later.

At the end of your LSDW session, you might have expanded the material, or you might have cut some material. Maybe both. But for purposes of this example, let's say you ended the week with ten pages of revised material, or around 2,500 words. That is one week's output in which you spent roughly six hours "training" or "working out" with your writing sessions. Do the math: over the course of forty weeks like this (about nine months) it's possible to have completed a book manuscript of up to 400 pages.

Now, of course, this is an idealized and perhaps oversimplified example. Individual results will vary; nevertheless, it's potentially doable and you can begin to see the possibilities of training and conditioning the creative mind in this way.

These are the basic writing workouts that will make you a *ChiWriter*. But knowing the basic workouts isn't quite enough to put them into effective practice, just as knowing the basic physical workouts aren't enough to make an endurance athlete.

You may have heard the saying, "If you fail to plan you plan to fail." This is true but it doesn't quite go far enough. Most people fail at whatever they say they want to achieve because they fail in one or more of three areas: 1) establishing a clear goal; 2) developing a plan to achieve that goal; and, 3) utilizing the proper tools, techniques, and strategies to follow through on that plan. They may be motivated to make a positive change in some area of their lives, but without clarity in any one or more of these areas, failure is far more likely.

For example, many people start off a new year with the resolution to "get in shape" so they join a gym. Most will fail in this resolution because "get in shape" is not a clear goal; simply joining a gym is not a plan; and it's likely they possess insufficient knowledge or understanding about tools, techniques, or strategies that can support their efforts.

It's the same with writing.

Many people say they want to write or they have a book inside them they want to get on the page, and they may be able to motivate themselves in the beginning but this quickly wanes when they realize how difficult it can be. Like the armchair athlete, they begin without a clear goal, a plan, or any strategies or techniques to support the plan.

In a situation like this, no matter the goal, the likely result is: the motivation they had in the beginning is quickly overcome by the discomfort involved in the physical and mental effort involved in changing established habits. They fail to break old patterns of behavior and soon abandon the goal and revert to the way of life they've become accustomed to, not because it moves them in the positive direction they say they want to go, but because it's easier, safer, more comfortable. They don't have to deal with the discomfort of change—even though this discomfort is temporary and wanes over time as progress is made toward the goal.

Near and present comfort is a powerful force that can easily counteract the motivation to change despite any future promise that change holds for you. And yet if you *want* something different than what you are currently experiencing you must *commit* to acting differently. Remember that what you want already exists for you within the energetic realm of pure potential—or else you would not have the desire to do it or even the slightest idea about it. But it remains only as potential unless you choose to manifest it through consistent thought (mental energy) and action (physical energy)—that involves a period of discomfort that must be endured.

That is why commitment is so important, as we discussed earlier. Commitment is much stronger than simple motivation because commitment is internal rather than external.

Commitment says "I will no matter what" whereas motivation says "I will as long as I feel like it." Commitment begets autotelic experience whereas motivation remains exotelic. Therefore, commitment is not as easily overcome as motivation. Commitment knows that discomfort must be endured for the greater good. Commitment, more than simple motivation, naturally seeks out the three primary ingredients of success: a clear goal, a plan, and techniques and strategies to support follow-through on that plan.

Key Planning and Training Principles

Endurance athletes, whether amateur or professional, use the following principles to meet their commitment to compete on race day and cross the finish line of their event. As you will see, all of these principles are applicable to the *ChiWriting* life and will help you successfully cross the finish line of your book.

Five principles apply to planning—developing a clear goal and a plan to get there—and five apply to training—the strategies and techniques that support your efforts and keep you on plan and moving forward. First, I will list the principles so you have a good idea of what they are at the outset. Then I'll go over each one in more detail in terms of how an athlete uses them, and explain how you can apply them to supercharge your writing life.

Five key planning principles:

1. **Define the major seasonal goal.** Athletes, in any sport, train by season (most often annually) and the major goal for the season is defined. The athlete has a definite primary event in mind as the major goal for the season, which means there is a specific future date (the event date) by which the athlete needs to be fully conditioned and ready to compete.

2. **Define interim seasonal goals.** Athletes frequently schedule interim events in order to qualify for a major event, or as a way of testing the efficacy of the training plan. For example, an athlete whose seasonal goal is to complete a full marathon might incorporate competition in shorter events—a 5K or 10K race—into her training plan to fine tuning race strategy, conditioning, and performance.

3. **Utilize "periodization."** Periodization structures training over specific periods or phases to ensure that conditioning

Part 2: The ChiWriting Principles

progresses appropriately and peaks at the most appropriate time.

4. **Develop a specific, written training plan.** The effective athlete will create a specific written seasonal/monthly/weekly/daily training plan utilizing specific workouts on a consistent basis in order to be sure she is ready to compete come race day. This plan is also important in tracking progress to ensure any necessary adjustments are made along the way.

5. **Have a goal for every single workout.** Once a complete overall plan is in place, athletes structure each individual workout to accomplish a specific goal that supports achievement of the overall desired outcome.

Five key training principles:

1. **Train consistently and frequently.** The endurance athlete knows that training the body and its energy systems consistently and frequently is a better path to success than focusing solely on the total volume (amount) of training. The endurance athlete knows she cannot simply train on weekends or wait until a few weeks out and then start training and expect to be successful on race day.

2. **Incorporate rest and recovery.** The endurance athlete knows that recovery—periods of rest, sleep, and less intensive physical effort (active recovery)—are as important as periods of focused physical training. He knows the body's adaptations to training only happen during recovery periods, when the body repairs and rebuilds.

3. **Utilize coaching and/or team support.** The endurance athlete recognizes the value of coaching and/or team-

based training. He knows that working with others and being accountable to others for his efforts keeps his commitment levels high. He knows that leveraging the support and expertise of others will further his goals more efficiently and powerfully.

4. **Train mentally as well as physically.** The endurance athlete utilizes mental training as well as physical training. She knows that mental conditioning is just as important as physical conditioning for success.

5. **Recognize the importance of diet and nutrition.** The endurance athlete knows that nutrition and diet is of the utmost importance in fueling the body properly for maintaining and enhancing the energy levels required of both training workouts and race competition.

Every professional or serious amateur endurance athlete uses these planning and training principles in some form or fashion. Knowing and consistently applying them are what distinguishes the successful athlete—those who actually cross their finish line—from armchair athletes who say that want to cross a finish line, but who lack the commitment to follow through, who only dabble and engage in half-hearted efforts, and who therefore give up far too easily.

Chances are, you can already begin to see how your writing life can be modeled on these principles to add tremendous value and productivity. But let's now discuss each one in more depth so you know specifically how to apply them to achieve that outcome.

Five Key Planning Principles

1. Define the major seasonal goal. Every professional team sport—baseball, football, basketball, hockey, soccer, etc.—has an annual "season." Baseball season, for example, runs from spring through the fall. Football season runs from the fall to mid-winter, and so on. In professional team sports, the major goal for the season is a foregone conclusion: every team wants to become the champions in their respective sport, whether that means winning the World Series, the Super Bowl, the NBA Championship, the World Cup for soccer, or the Stanley Cup in hockey.

Professional endurance athletes also train with a major goal in mind. Serious Ironman athletes want to compete in the World Championships in Kona, Hawaii each year. Serious marathon runners want to qualify for and compete in a major event like the Boston Marathon. Even amateurs tend to have a major event they are training for and complete.

So every endurance athlete, whether professional or amateur, has a definite primary event in mind as the major goal for the season, which means there is a specific future date (the event date) by which the athlete needs to be fully conditioned and ready to compete. The period of time between that major race goal and when training to achieve that goal begins can be defined as that athlete's "season."

In my case, I wanted to complete the Ironman Louisville race, and I trained specifically for that race over a period of nine months. Those nine months became my "season" and completing the race became my own personal championship.

Thinking in terms of seasons gives the endurance athlete a number of planning advantages: it puts a long-term perspective into your planning. It plants a firmly aspirational goal in the athlete's consciousness that keeps her inspired to continue moving forward, even on those days when she doesn't feel like working out, because she knows if she doesn't workout she will not be properly conditioned to meet her goal come race day. Defining a "season" also lends a natural structure to the training plan. Knowing the start date (when training begins) and the end date (when the major event take place) enables the athlete to more easily develop a written training plan and apply the other components of plan development, such as defining interim goals and utilizing periodization, etcetera.

How this Principle Applies to Your Writing. Now let's take a look at this principle and see how you might apply it to your writing life in order to cross the finish line of a book or other writing project. First of all, to apply a seasonal outlook to your writing, you first must have a goal to shoot for. Again, for a marathon runner, the seasonal goal might be completing the Boston Marathon; for a triathlete, the Kona Championships; for a football player, the Super Bowl, etcetera. For your writing, you might say you want to complete a novel in time to submit it to a competition and the deadline for submitting a manuscript for that competition is nine or ten months away. That is your seasonal goal. That is the "championship" event you want to be ready for.

Setting an aspirational goal like this accomplishes two things right away: first it establishes a concrete end date for your training and efforts that immediately begins to add vital structure to your writing life. You know what you're shooting for so you're far less likely to feel like you are flailing away for no good reason when the work is difficult (and it will be difficult sometimes). Second, a worthy long-term goal is far more likely to keep you committed to following through on your plan. Remember that commitment is more important than simple motivation, as we discussed earlier.

Setting a seasonal goal immediately focuses your efforts. You know what you are shooting for. As Stephen Covey put it in his best-selling book *7 Habits of Highly Effective People*, you "begin with the end in mind." This is key to organizing and calibrating your writing life. An endurance athlete who is not training for a specific event is less likely to stick to a focused training plan.

Similarly, if, as a writer, you don't have an end goal in mind, you are far less likely to stick to a focused "training" plan that moves you forward in your writing. When I was training for an Ironman race, there were days when I just did not feel like training. But I knew if I did not, I would not progress enough in my physical and mental conditioning to be ready on race day. Having that end goal in mind, and knowing that I needed to progress to meet that goal, spurred me on despite initial reluctance on any particular day.

And no matter how busy I was or how much I didn't want to work out on any given day, when it was over, I was always glad I did it anyway. Not only did it move me further down the path to my ultimate goal, it energized me mentally and physically—no matter how tired I was after a long work out of biking, running, or swimming, I always felt good for having accomplished that particular workout. Those positive feelings reinforced my commitment to my end goal.

This same principle also applied to me during my writing life in the MFA program at Spalding University. There, the "season" was two years (since it was a two-year program) and the goal—the ultimate event I was shooting for, my personal championship—was graduating with my MFA degree (and in the process complete a book-length manuscript). Having that end in mind at the beginning was key to focusing my efforts every step along the way because I knew that if I didn't get the work done—if I didn't train (read and write) nearly every day—I'd fall behind in my creative conditioning and the end goal would be impossible to achieve.

How long should your season be?

First, remember that the whole idea of organizing around a "season" is that there is also an off-season, which is meant to provide time to rest, recover, and reenergize before the next season starts—more about that later. With that in mind I'd recommend a writing season of at least nine to ten months, which will give you a good chunk of time to organize and develop a training plan and get a good amount of work done while also allowing a nice off-season to recharge, reflect, and enjoy your accomplishments.

Let's say you want to participate in National Novel Writing Month (NaNoWriMo), which occurs each November and encourages participants to complete a novel in a month's time. Who says you have to wait until November to begin? If you want to complete a book by the end of November, you could use NaNoWriMo as your seasonal goal. You could begin in January and structure a training plan to complete a manuscript by October 31 and then spend the month of November polishing and refining your work.

What if your book can't possibly be finished in a single season? That's okay; it's perfectly fine to structure your training plan across more than one season, if necessary. Look at Olympic athletes — their major event competition occurs every four years, so they structure their training over a four-year period to ensure optimal conditioning and readiness for that event — including annual goals such as championships in their particular event and qualifying Olympic Trials.

So if you have a lengthy work in mind — say you want to write a long historical novel or nonfiction work that requires a lot of intensive research — you may want to devote a significant portion of your first season of training to research. Simply build that phase into your plan and extend your plan across two or more seasons, as appropriate. I'll have more to say about this when discussing the written training plan and periodization below.

2. Define interim "seasonal" goals. Just as every athlete — whether an individual endurance athlete or member of a sports team — has a major seasonal goal, so too do they have interim goals they want to achieve. A sports team must first qualify for the playoffs, then win a league or conference championship before having a chance to achieve their major goal. A marathon runner must place well in other races in order to qualify for the Boston Marathon. An Ironman athlete also must compete in other races as a way of qualifying for the Ironman Championship in Kona, Hawaii.

Part 2: The ChiWriting Principles

There is always a single major goal, but there is never *just* a single major goal; along the way, athletes also complete smaller interim goals that prepare them to complete the big one.

There are several major advantages to this.

First, it creates shorter-term goals that keep commitment and confidence high for continuing and completing daily training. A long-term goal is just that—long-term. Relatively speaking it's a long way off and trying to keep your energy focused at a target so distant can be difficult. Interim goals allow the athlete to set her sights on a target that's a bit easier to see. The pathway from here to there is shorter, so she can see her way there more clearly. That keeps her mentally aligned and focused.

Second, scheduling interim events is an excellent method of testing the efficacy of the training plan, to gauge how conditioning is progressing; it also enables the athlete to practice and fine tune race strategy and performance for the big goal. Is the training plan working? Am I making enough progress with my physical conditioning? These are the questions completing an interim goal will answer. Let's say an aspiring athlete is training to complete a marathon in less than four hours; completing an actual 10K race or half-marathon during training is an excellent way to determine if that goal is on track.

Third, it gives the athlete experience with actual race day dynamics—mentally, race day is a much different experience, with a different energy and dynamic, than training alone or with a small group.

Fourth, completing interim goals give athletes a significant confidence boost that injects new energy and enthusiasm into efforts. When I was training to complete my Ironman race, that was my major "seasonal" goal, my "A" race, my overarching objective; yet, part of my plan to get there also included competing in several shorter running races and triathlons. Gaining this experience in actual shorter races contributed significantly to achieving my greater goal. Would it have been possible to achieve without competing in a few shorter events first? Sure, it would have been possible. But it also would have been more difficult to believe in my capability, and I would have approached the main event with much less confidence.

And here's the other thing: when you have a goal so far in the distance, you tend to think you have plenty of time to reach it; that mindset tends to lead you down the pathway of thinking that you can slack off in your day-to-day training because there's still "plenty of time" to get in shape for the big event. That may be true in isolated cases, but the danger is that you risk slipping into a lackadaisical routine that leaves you unprepared for the event.

Scheduling interim goals encourages a mindset that day-to-day training is imperative because you want to be ready for those shorter events as well. Completing shorter events/goals gives you greater confidence that will inhibit the tendency to slack off; when you slack off, physical conditioning gains are lost because the body constantly adapts to its inputs. A lot of activity will result in greater conditioning as the body adapts; but if then the activity stops, the conditioning will stop and the body will adapt negatively, reverting to a level of deconditioning that corresponds to the reduced level of activity.

How this Principle Applies to Your Writing. Setting out to accomplish any big goal can seem daunting. It may even seem impossible at the outset, so impossible you may not even attempt it. Isn't that why you haven't written your book yet? You want to, but you haven't. Why? Because it seems impossible.

You're too busy, there's not enough time. You're not sure you have the talent. You've tried and you just can't get started, staring at that blank page. If you have so much trouble just getting a single page written, how are you going to fill a book's worth of pages? So you give up, or you don't try at all. Many people have the same thoughts about getting fit; they know they want to, they know they'll feel better about themselves if they do, but it seems impossible, the work and effort required is too daunting. Not doing anything is so much easier.

Many, many people opt for easier. And that's okay—there's no judgment here. But if you've set that major goal, if you have your personal championship in mind, you must be prepared to do the hard work, to take the more difficult path, and that most likely will entail some discomfort. But, again, the creative mind adapts just like the physical body does. If it is pushed, it responds and it may seem very difficult at first; it may seem like you're going nowhere fast, but as your creative mind adapts and becomes more conditioned, it will become easier.

That's why it's important to set smaller goals on the way to your big goal. When you accomplish smaller goals, you get the satisfaction and gratification—positive energy—that keeps driving you forward toward your larger goal. To return to the previous planning principle, when you begin with the end in mind and define your major goal, take a step back and define a couple of interim goals that are a bit easier to see and which keep your inspiration and sense of accomplishment high; that test the efficacy of your writing regimen and mirror the dynamics of finishing the complete book, which gives you a significant confidence boost that injects new energy into your writing program.

There are a couple of different ways to do this. Since you are writing a book, you could adapt a portion of it into a shorter work and submit it to an appropriate market. For example, if you are writing a novel and your major seasonal goal is to submit the novel to an agent (a goal you will plan in advance), then you could also research short story markets and plan to submit a shorter, self-contained excerpt to a short story contest—there are many out there. If you are writing a book of poetry, you could submit a few poems to journals as a regular interim goal. If you are writing a non-fiction book, you could take your subject matter, adapt a shorter article and submit it to an appropriate market—a journal, a newspaper, even a blog.

The idea is to get the sense of a win, of completion, of accomplishment, on a smaller scale than your major goal so that you know you really are progressing and moving forward. But don't get hung up on actual publication: for one thing, you're not likely to hear back from a potential market for a while—perhaps months—and you've got to keep moving and training. For another thing, you're not likely to get any substantive feedback from the markets you are submitting to beyond either a simple rejection or acceptance; and the odds are overwhelmingly in favor of the former no matter how good the work is. The idea is simply to get pieces of your writing out there; when you click send, or drop a manuscript in the mailbox, that is crossing a finish line. That is your interim event.

The other way is to read your work aloud to a small group or share it with a small group or trusted friend or writing coach. If you belong to a writing group or are connected in some way to a community of writers, part of your overall plan should be to get your writing out in front of these compatriots over the course of your writing season (more about coaches and writing groups in the next section). If you are looking for feedback, this is a far better way of getting it than submitting it somewhere for publication. And if you find the feedback valuable, so much the better.

But the main objective is not the feedback itself. The main objective is to set smaller goals that help you achieve the big one, your major seasonal goal. The value here is in setting interim deadlines—*I will submit to journals by this date*, or *I will send this to my writing group by this date*—and working to meet those deadlines.

Many writers feel they have to keep the book they are working on under wraps, until they feel it's "finished." But the truth is, it may never "feel" finished if you keep it under wraps. The experience of "finishing" a portion of the larger work, by preparing it for submission either to a writing market or writing group or coach, helps to circumvent the tendency to rework material over and over such that very little overall progress is made.

3. Utilize "periodization." We've talked about having a specific end goal in mind, and about planning smaller, interim goals as a way of maintaining momentum and testing yourself. Another important concept from the field of endurance training is "periodization": a way of systematically planning a training program over time to ensure optimal conditioning and performance for the most important event of the year (the seasonal goal). It structures training over specific blocks of time (periods) to ensure that conditioning progresses consistently and peaks at the most appropriate time.

For example, over a season-long training period leading up to a major race, an endurance athlete may structure training in four basic periods or phases:

1. *General preparation training,* in which workouts are focused on building a foundational level of fitness;

2. *Base training,* in which workouts are focused on building specific aspects of fitness, such as strength or speed;

3. *Build training,* in which workouts are focused on building race- or sport-specific aspects of fitness, such as power and endurance; and,

4. *Peak training,* in which workouts are focused on optimizing fitness and energy levels for race day, typically including a "taper" period during which the overall volume of training is reduced to ensure the body is adequately adapted and prepared for actual race day-demands.

Many athletes and coaches think in terms of "cycles" when periodizing a training plan: a *microcycle* is the shortest period, usually around one week; a *mesocycle* is a group of microcycles, usually up to several weeks; and, a *macrocycle* is a group of mesocycles, lasting up to several months. So a typical periodized plan would include three or four macrocycles, each consisting of mesocycles, which in turn consist of several microcycles.

The microcycles would consist of specific daily workouts of various types and with varying levels of intensities and volumes, along with, of course, recovery periods. If this all sounds quite complicated, it needn't be; it's simply a way of structuring training so the athlete knows what she must accomplish during any given phase or cycle.

The goal of periodization is to be in peak conditioning at the time of the main event. The focus of each cycle, or phase, is on building specific aspects of physical conditioning. During the first several weeks of a training plan, for example, the athlete might focus on general preparation, that is, conditioning the body and its systems (aerobic, anaerobic, muscular) to prepare it for more intense effort or greater volume in later cycles. This foundational level of conditioning also helps protect against injury.

Following the preparatory phase, later cycles might focus on workouts specifically designed to increase base levels of strength (the muscles' ability to produce force) and speed (pushing the lactate, or anaerobic, threshold up). The focus of the build phase might be improving endurance (the ability to sustain long-term effort); and finally, the peak phase might be a period of refining aspects of fitness and conditioning to ensure optimum race-day performance. This phase would typically include a "taper" period, in which volume of exercise is dialed down a bit, while maintaining intensity, to give the body a chance to fully recover and adapt to the training regimen in order to ensure peak energy at race time.

Part 2: The ChiWriting Principles

In each of these phases the same three basic workouts we discussed earlier are used, but they are combined in a variety of ways throughout a microcycle and performed at varying levels of intensity, duration, and volume, depending on the overall goal of the phase (or period) and the individual workout itself (more about individual workouts later). Essentially, intensity, duration, and volume are all manipulated over time to produce the body's necessary adaptations.

The off-season — the period following accomplishment of the seasonal goal and before the next season starts — might also be considered a planning phase. Having accomplished her seasonal goal, the endurance athlete utilizes an off-season period to rest and recover, while maintaining a less rigorous training plan. Such a period allows the athlete to refocus, recharge, reenergize, and plan the next season's training and events.

How this Principle Applies to Your Writing. To see how valuable the concept of periodization can be to your writing life, consider how many would-be writers typically approach the creation of their manuscript: with a goal to write a book — perhaps an idea for the book — but no real plan for how to achieve that goal. Without that plan, they sit down to get started and quickly find that forward progress is not as easy as they imagined. Soon, they give up in frustration. The same thing happens to people who want to get in better physical shape, but have no real plan to accomplish that. They may have good intentions at the start — they may go out one morning and begin to walk or run or bike — but they quickly realize how difficult it can be, how out of shape they are, how much time and effort is really going to be involved in properly conditioning their bodies, and they quickly revert to sitting on the couch.

Periodization helps overcome this tendency by creating a structure for training — it is not the training plan itself, but it provides a framework in which to place the training, enabling you to envision how your conditioning will progress and, importantly, taking initial unrealistic expectations out of the equation.

What do I mean by that? Starting out with any long-term goal—whether getting in shape, writing a book, or something else—most people have an unrealistic expectation that they will perform in the beginning as if they have been working out or writing for a long time, as if they are already conditioned. When they realize that is not the case, they tend to give up easily. This is where periodization can help.

The first phase of most periodization plans is the general preparation phase, in which the athlete first prepares or pre-conditions the body for the more intense phases to come. Activities in this preparatory phase strengthen the muscles, tendons, and ligaments to prepare them to perform at higher levels later without injury; it begins to strengthen the aerobic system, increasing the lactate threshold and thereby increasing the body's workload capacity. Activities during the general preparation phase also build the habits and rituals necessary to sustain training in later phases that demand more of the body.

This same preparatory level of conditioning—again the first phase of a periodized plan—is also vital for the writer. The writer must prepare the creative mind for the more intense phases to come. When I decided to apply for the MFA program, for example, I first entered a preparatory training phase in which I began to read more and write more, conditioning my creative mind and building the habits, routines, rituals, and processes necessary to sustain what I knew would be much more intense rigors of the two-year MFA program.

For me, the general preparation period of creative conditioning lasted two years. I read more and wrote more for two years before I felt I was ready to begin an MFA program—before my creative conditioning progressed to the point where I felt I could be successful. If I had not spent this period in preparatory training, I likely would not have been accepted into the program and even if I had been, I likely would not have succeeded.

During my MFA program, I completed a book-length manuscript over a two-year period consisting of four semesters (two each year); each of these semester phases had its own structure and goals that built upon one another and progressively improved my creative conditioning, built my creative output, and prepared me for graduation (my main event). In other words, without realizing it at the time, my MFA program was structured utilizing phases of creative conditioning which can be considered analogous to endurance training periodization.

You can apply this same concept to your writing life to develop a structured plan that systematically moves your book project forward toward completion. A periodized writing plan using endurance training periodization as a model might look something like this:

- **General Preparation:** Performing necessary research into the idea, topic, or area of interest; developing the dramatic or narrative concept; creating an outline or overall structure for the book; establishing characters, conflicts, settings, mapping out plots/subplots, etc.

- **Base Training:** Fleshing out the concept and/or outline; focusing on generating the raw material for your book, developing characters and plotlines; getting words on the page that you can then work with.

- **Build Training:** Further developing, and deepening the raw material; focusing on rewriting previous material and expanding with new material where needed; building out a complete manuscript.

- **Peak Training:** Rewriting and refining your manuscript; further revisions as necessary, including a "taper" period focused on line edits and polishing the overall work.

Without this periodized structure, writing a book can seem overwhelming to the point where a would-be writer gives up in frustration after making little overall progress over time, or, in some cases, fails to even start. The structure of periodization allows you to move forward in a systematic way, utilizing blocks of time over weeks or months to accomplish goals step-by-step; time devoted to the writing project is invested efficiently and productively; progress can be more easily tracked, and therefore, corrections and adjustments to the plan can be made more easily.

And like the endurance athlete, structuring a writing plan like this enables you to also utilize an off-season period following accomplishment of the seasonal goal to rest and recover, maintaining a less rigorous writing regimen until the new season starts, to enable the creative mind to adapt, recharge, and reenergize. This off-season period also allows you time to plan the next season's writing training and goals. If your book is completed within a single season, you use this time to plan the next season's book. If your book is still in progress at the end of your season, you use this period to assess and plan how to move forward toward completion when a new season begins.

4. Develop a specific, written training plan. Having a written plan with clearly defined goals and steps is helpful for achieving any long-term objective. But for the endurance athlete, it's absolutely essential. To illustrate this, imagine first what it would be like to train without a goal or a plan. Imagine that you only have a vague notion that you want to run a marathon "someday," for example. You don't know which one or when it will be, so you don't have an end goal in mind with a specific timeframe — your "season" is not defined; therefore, there is no organizing framework for your efforts; you just decide that someday you will run a marathon and so you begin running.

You run awhile on that first day and it's hard; you struggle. You tell yourself it's okay, you knew it would be hard. The next day, your muscles are very sore so you decide to take it easy a couple of days to let your body recover. You plan to run again a couple days later. But then a deadline at work comes up and the run you had planned gets pushed aside. No problem, you think, you'll make up for it on the weekend. You try to run harder and longer on the weekend and it's even more of a struggle. You begin to think it's never going to happen, you won't have the time it takes, you'll never be able to get in the physical condition that's required. When that kind of thinking takes over, it's usually only a matter of time before you give up. This is how many people approach training, and it helps explain why many people give up after a short time.

Anyone serious about completing a marathon—or achieving any long-term goal—would never approach it in such an unfocused, slipshod manner. When "someday" is your timeframe and the training is accomplished only when you can find the time or when you feel like it, failure is the likely result.

Now look at the opposite approach. Let's say you're at the finish line of a marathon in your hometown in late October; you're there to cheer a friend on. The atmosphere of the race and the crowd is electric and exciting as runners cross the finish line. Then you see your friend; you start cheering her on, you're excited for her as she crosses the finish line—she did it! You congratulate her. What an accomplishment!

You think, if your friend can do it, so can you, so you make the decision right then and there to complete in next year's race. You've made the decision. Now what? Well, you've already taken two important steps: you've defined the end goal and you've defined the length of your season—you have the next twelve months to train and prepare yourself and you know the exact date you will be crossing the finish line.

The next step is to write down your training plan—what you will do every day to ensure you are physically and mentally ready to complete that race come next October. Writing down your training plan is a critical step to success. A written training plan essentially enables you to break your big goal down into a series of smaller goals—your periodized phases and your daily workouts. It's much easier to focus on simply completing each day's training rather than focusing solely on the big goal, which could seem overwhelming.

Over time, as your body adapts to the training and conditioning improves—and the day of the race gets closer—you begin to see and feel the improvement in your body, in your endurance, in your aerobic capacity; and you begin to see and feel that it is possible to cross that finish line as your friend did. The momentum and energy created by completing each day's training—by focusing only on that small goal—pulls you toward the big goal.

How this Principle Applies to Your Writing. It may seem counterintuitive to have a written "training" plan for writing a book; after all, it's a creative process that's not subject to the rules and stricture of a "plan," right? Not really. The way to look at it, as I've said before, is that the creative mind is a muscle that needs to be exercised in order to grow and develop, just like the physical body does. And just like physical muscles, the creative mind will respond to stimulus. It cannot *not* respond.

Regularly training the creative mind and pushing it beyond its current limits, will force it to adapt and become much more efficient and effective, just as physical training forces the body to adapt. To illustrate, let's look at the same scenario as above, just from a writing perspective.

Part 2: The ChiWriting Principles

Imagine first what it would be like to try and write a book without a goal or a plan. You want to write a book "someday," for example. You have an idea for a book but it's not fully developed and you don't know when you'll complete it (or when you'll find the time to complete it), so you don't have an end goal in mind with a specific timeframe—your "season" is not defined; therefore there is no organizing framework for your efforts; you only know that someday you will finish your book, so with all good intentions you sit down one day and begin writing.

You write for awhile on that first day and it's harder than expected; you struggle. You tell yourself it's okay, you knew it would be hard. The next day, you sit down to write again, but it's still hard; you can't figure out how to express your ideas and the words won't come. You may find yourself going over and over the same passage or even the same sentence. Then a deadline at work comes up and the writing you had planned to do gets pushed aside. No problem, you think, you'll make up for it on the weekend when you have more time. You try to write harder and longer on the weekend and it's even more of a struggle. You begin to think it's never going to happen, you won't have the time it takes, you'll never be able to get on the page the words required. When that kind of thinking takes over, it's usually only a matter of time before you give up.

This is how most people who want to write a book approach it—without a real plan; and just like people who want and try to get in shape without a plan, it helps explain why most people give up after a short time.

You can say you have a commitment to writing a book, but what is the foundation for that commitment without a written plan? A written plan undergirds your commitment, gives it a framework upon which to build. That framework supports your commitment and makes it much more likely you'll succeed.

With a plan in place your energies are gathered, focused, and channeled, not inchoate, scattered, and dissipated. With a plan in place, you know exactly what's expected of you each day, which makes it far more likely that you will follow through. You know the end goal—you've begun with the end in mind, as Covey wrote—but with a plan in place to get you there, your focus is not on the faraway but on the day-to-day. To reach your goal you only need to do what's required in your plan on any given day. These daily accomplishments build upon one another, giving you momentum and greater confidence each step of the way.

5. Plan weekly and have a goal for every single workout. Once a complete overall plan is in place, taking into account seasonal and interim goals and periodization, endurance athletes structure weekly plans down to each individual daily workout to accomplish a specific goal that supports achievement of the overall desired outcome.

First, the athlete plans his season; he knows what his overall goal is; he's defined a few interim goals to keep himself on track; he has periodized his plan, too; that is, structured it in phases to ensure consistent progress—and he knows what he wants to accomplish during that particular block of training. The next step is to break it down to weekly and daily goals. He might have a weekly volume goal (the total time devoted to training), and that volume might consist of workouts of varying levels of intensity. Then he looks at each day of the week and decides what he is going to do each day to get to his desired goal. Remember the three types of workouts covered earlier? The athlete is going to know which of these types of workouts to do any given day of the week, and for how long, and for what purpose.

If an athlete is training for a marathon and has a weekly volume goal of thirty miles of running during the base training phase, how is she going to reach that weekly goal? She is going to plan out her week, focusing on what type of workout to do each day. For example:

- On Tuesday, Thursday, and Saturday, she may plan to complete thirty-minute workouts of two miles each using high intensity intervals (six miles and ninety minutes total);
- On Wednesday and Friday, she will complete one hour, six-mile tempo runs (twelve miles and two hours total);
- On Sunday, she will complete a long, slow distance run of two hours or about twelve miles;
- On Monday, she would rest and recover.

This weekly plan would achieve the total volume goal of twelve miles with a total time commitment of less than six hours, and each workout trains the body in a different way to accomplish specific conditioning goals. She planned out what she was going to do each day, making it far more likely that she would actually follow through, and her plan was time-efficient, meaning she was able to meet her weekly conditioning goals while still maintaining her ability to fulfill her other important life responsibilities, such as work and family obligations.

The time efficiency of her plan also allows enough flexibility to adapt and respond to unforeseen circumstances and still accomplish her weekly volume goal. The three shorter, high intensity interval workouts, for example, could be completed in thirty minutes or less, enabling her to easily fit them into a busy schedule, morning, midday, or evening, depending on what is happening on any given day.

How this Principle Applies to Your Writing. Most people who want to write a book fantasize about chucking their jobs and devoting all day to their writing efforts. But most people —

including most working, publishing writers—can't afford that luxury. Chances are, you can't devote six hours a day to your writing. But with a time-efficient weekly and daily plan, it is possible to invest six hours per week in your writing, even if you are already extremely busy with work, family, and other personal obligations. And with those six weekly hours, it is possible to be productive and make substantial progress on your book over your planned "season."

How do you do this? You develop a weekly plan based on your periodization goals, just as the endurance athlete does in our example above, and you make every writing workout count by utilizing each of the three writing workouts previous discussed— High Intensity Writing, Tempo Writing, and Long, Slow Writing to vary the intensities of the workouts and enable different types of creative conditioning.

Let's say you work a demanding schedule Monday through Friday. Can you squeeze in thirty minutes of writing four days a week in the mornings before work or in the evenings before bed? That is two hours. On the weekends, can you squeeze in a longer session of two hours each on Saturday and Sunday? That is six hours total for the week, in which it is possible to generate eight to ten pages of material, depending on the writing workouts. When we break down that six hours a week into shorter daily writing workouts, the weekly goal begins to be much more manageable, and you are conditioning your creative mind in a much more efficient way that will lead to greater productivity overall—more about this in the next section.

Five Key Training Principles

1. Train consistently and frequently. You've probably heard of a "weekend warrior," a person who is sedentary throughout the week and then goes overboard on the weekend with physical activity in an attempt to make up for lost time. This doesn't work.

This is a recipe for lack of progress, injury, and, at the very least, weekly soreness and muscle aches. It is much better to be physically active for shorter periods consistently and frequently throughout the week.

An example: say you want to complete a marathon. You know you must train for it, so you plan to devote six hours a week to training. But you are busy during the week, so your plan is to run for six hours over the weekend, when you have more time. Is this a good plan? Probably not.

The key to making conditioning gains is progressive overload. This concept means that, to grow, an athlete must overload his muscles and/or aerobic system, which then provokes an adaptation response—the body responds and adapts to this stimulus by becoming stronger and fitter in order to handle the increased workload. This is done over and over so that the adaptation (i.e., conditioning) is progressive and thus continually improving.

But attempting to provoke this adaptation response all at once by cramming six hours of training into one or two sessions per week is counterproductive. The body is overwhelmed. You are far more likely to injure yourself. You are far less likely to get the progressive conditioning you need in order to complete over twenty-six miles of continuous running to meet your goal of crossing the finish line of a marathon.

Yet, it is possible to train successfully for a marathon in only six hours per week. You do it by dividing that six hours into more frequent, shorter training sessions consistently performed. During the week, you might train for twenty to thirty minutes using high intensity intervals—pushing your body to its limits for short periods, then recovering for a short period, then repeating that cycle six or eight times. Do that two or three times a week. (That's about an hour to an hour and a half). For another two days a week, you run perhaps forty-five minutes, but during these workouts you use tempo intervals, running at just under full capacity for longer intervals of ten to fifteen minutes, with recovery periods in between. That's another hour and a half.

So over the course of a typical workweek, you've trained about three hours total. That leaves you three hours of training time over a weekend, which you could accomplish with a long, slow easy run in two, hour and a half sessions, or later on perhaps one, three-hour session. That is a total of six hours of training per week, with one or two days of rest and recovery, depending on your plan.

This plan incorporates consistency and frequency into the training regimen using the three types of workouts discussed earlier. This is a much more efficient way of conditioning your body to meet your goal. Using this methodology, you will progressively condition your body, its muscles and aerobic systems, while protecting against injury. Consistency and frequency in training is far more effective and efficient than trying to cram the same amount of training into one or two sessions.

How this Principle Applies to Your Writing. This same methodology, and the reasons it works, also applies to your writing and your goal of completing a book. It is why it's important to plan out your weekly writing workouts and know exactly what you want to accomplish on any given day. As we talked about above, some writers have the luxury of being able to sit down to write six hours a day. Most writers do not have that luxury (and even if they do, it's difficult to sit and write for that long). So how can you make the time you do have to write most effective and efficient? The answer is to divide the time you can devote to writing to shorter, more frequent and consistent writing sessions, rather that one or two longer sessions.

Like the weekend warrior, the weekend writer is simply far less likely to achieve the progress needed to reach her goals. Similar to the example above, let's say you plan to write for six hours per week to achieve your goal of writing a book. Trying to cram that six hours of writing into one or two sessions a week can be as counterproductive for the writer as it is to the athlete, and for many of the same reasons: the creative mind responds and adapts to increased workloads just as the body does, but longer, infrequent writing sessions do not train and condition the creative mind as effectively as shorter and more frequent sessions; the creative mind is more likely to be overwhelmed, stalling progress.

You may find yourself staring too long at a blank page, reworking the same line over and over, or listening too soon to your overly critical internal editor. Infrequent writing sessions also make it more difficult to build consistency of habit. In a way, not writing over the course of a workweek and then trying to catch up on Saturday or Sunday is like starting from scratch every weekend.

It is far more efficient to divide that writing time into shorter sessions throughout the week, rather than trying to cram it into one or two longer sessions over a weekend — you are conditioning your creative mind much more effectively. During the week, devote three hours to writing by dividing the time into four, fifteen-minute high-intensity sessions (one hour) and two tempo sessions of up to an hour each (two hours). For the high-intensity sessions, your focus is on writing non-stop, as quickly as you can.

The goal is to get raw material on the page without overthinking it or getting your internal editor too involved too early. For the longer tempo sessions, you focus on quickly rewriting what you wrote, expanding as you go along, without editing too much; if you pick up an interesting thread of thought, you pick up the intensity a bit and just get the words down on paper. On the weekend, you then have three hours for a long, slow writing session, during which you work the material you have developed at a slower pace, rewriting where necessary, revising everywhere, editing, correcting, shaping the raw material into a more finished form. You can do this in a single three-hour session, or divide the time into two, ninety-minute sessions.

I recommend you devote a minimum of six hours weekly to a "training" plan for your writing; with this methodology, you may find you can even expand the time you have available to write from six to eight or nine hours — particularly once your creative mind is "in shape," i.e., conditioned to write. When your creative mind is conditioned to write, you may find that it becomes an autotelic experience, that you enjoy it so you want and need to devote more time — just as an athlete whose body is conditioned comes to enjoy the feel and satisfaction of working out for its own sake.

If you have less time than six hours in any given week, that's fine too; the key is to keep a consistent, frequent training schedule. A key rule of thumb to keep in mind is: the less time you have available, the more intense your workout sessions should be. If an endurance athlete only has fifteen minutes for a workout, she is going to go with a high-intensity interval training session, which is going to push her body to the limits in a short time, giving her conditioning benefits in a very time-efficient manner.

Similarly, if as a writer you only have fifteen minutes to devote to your writing on any given day, make it count by making it a high-intensity writing session — put pen to paper or fingers to keyboard and don't stop writing for fifteen minutes. Don't stop to correct; don't stop to edit. This will give you creative conditioning benefits in a very time-efficient manner. It will push your creative mind to the limit, shut down your critical internal editor (since it's not needed at that point), and train your creative mind to more easily enter the flow state. If you do this, you will have at least two pages of raw material per workout — you can then go back and rework and revise the material using tempo and long, slow writing workouts when you have time.

2. Incorporate rest and recovery. An absolutely essential component of physical training is *not* training; that is, the endurance athlete must incorporate periods of rest, sleep, and less intensive physical effort to allow the body to recover properly from physical training. Pushing the body to its limits and beyond actually causes damage to muscles and tissues—it is the body's effort to repair this damage that leads to gains in physical conditioning. Increasing the lactate threshold, developing muscle strength and size, enhancing aerobic capacity and endurance—these things happen *after* training, during the recovery periods between workout sessions. Training tears down; recovery builds back up so that the athlete is better, stronger, faster than before as the body adapts. And these gains are cumulative and progressive, leading to gradual and greater improvement over time.

When physically training, the athlete is not consciously aware of how her body is adapting—it is an unconscious (or subconscious) process. She cannot consciously direct the bodily processes necessary for adaptation to physical stimuli—the cellular changes, the repair and growth of muscle tissue, the expansion of capillary blood flow and the enhancement of aerobic capacity and stamina—all of this happens without her conscious input (this is the life force working within her, another manifestation of chi). She can, however, consciously and positively influence these processes by fueling the body properly (discussed below) and by investing adequate time away from actual physical training.

The endurance athlete must factor rest and recovery into her planning at all levels, including her overall seasonal plan, her training phases, her weekly training schedule, and her planned daily workouts. For example, if her planned daily workout includes high intensity intervals, recovery periods are incorporated between intervals; in her weekly schedule she includes one day of rest with no planned workouts; for every three or four weeks of intensive or high volume training, she might plan one week of training in which intensity level or volume is dialed down a bit; and following her season, she might incorporate an "off-season," in which she takes a break from regular training and engages in other types of physical activities to refresh and reenergize.

How this Principle Applies to Your Writing. Conditioning the creative mind requires focused effort aimed at expanding current limits to stimulate growth and move the writer beyond her comfort zone, just as the endurance athlete uses focused effort to stimulate growth and condition the body for greater athletic performance. This means that writing, i.e., creative effort, requires that same "recovery" time.

When you are away from actual writing, not consciously thinking about your book, your subconscious mind is still working, still adapting to the creative stimulus, growing and conditioning your creative mind to better enable it to perform, to solve problems, to meet the storytelling challenges that yet face you. But to do that, to allow the subconscious creative mind to grow and adapt, requires time away from actual writing.

Many writers either feel guilty about time invested away from writing, like they should be doing more, or they feel that if they can't spend six or eight hours a day writing then they shouldn't bother, and they allow the many daily demands and obligations of living to swallow up any writing time at all.

But as a writer, embracing the principle that your creative mind needs "recovery" time to allow it to adapt to the training stimuli from writing workouts, just as the athlete needs to allow the body to recover from its physical training, means that time spent away from your writing is valuable and, in fact, necessary for your writing life.

This means that time spent in play, in quiet reflection, in reading, in sleep, in recreation, in enjoying meals and time with your loved ones, in pursuing the quotidian tasks of daily living, even in meeting the demands of whatever job you may have, is all valuable for the writer. So there is no need to feel guilty about not being able to invest more time at the page, nor is there any reason to give up altogether because you can't devote as much time as you'd like to your writing. It's all part of the creative process.

When creatively training, the writer is not consciously aware of how her creative mind is adapting to her writing workouts. Like the athlete's physiological adaptations, it is an unconscious (or subconscious) process. She cannot consciously direct the processes necessary for adaptation to creative stimuli—the cellular changes in the brain that strengthen synaptic connections between neurons and create new neural pathways enabling greater access to the energetic field of pure potential where her book resides.

This happens without her conscious input through the life force working within her. Like the athlete, however, she can positively influence these processes by consciously fueling the body properly, by exercising to improve overall energy levels, and by investing adequate time away from actual writing to allow creative adaptation and growth.

For the endurance athlete, training time isn't just the time invested in the actual physical workout—training time is actually twenty-four/seven; which means the time spent outside actual physical workouts is just as important as the workouts themselves because it supports the physical effort and the overall performance goal.

This is a key takeaway concept for the writer as well: *you are not a writer just when you are sitting down and actually writing; you are a writer all the time.* I'll have more to say about this later, but for now, begin to understand the mindset that as a writer, you are constantly "in training," not just the time actually spent at the page, but twenty-four/seven, because everything outside the time actually spent writing supports and enhances your overall creative performance goal.

3. Utilize coaching and/or team support. Endurance athletes compete alone. During a race, there is no one else out there who can run for them, no one else who can help them. When they cross the finish line, they cross alone, it's their achievement. But endurance athletes, especially elite professionals, have people supporting them. They may cross the finish line alone, but they do not accomplish that finish alone. The committed endurance athlete recognizes the value of coaching, team-based training, and/or other supportive relationships in achieving their goals.

When I was much younger, I watched a Wimbledon tennis match on television and was surprised to hear the announcers identify a man watching from the stands as a player's coach. If the player was so good, I wondered, why does he need a coach? I had thought of coaches as only necessary for team sports to call plays, coordinate the efforts of the players, and blow whistles during practice. At the time, it never occurred to me that athletes who competed as individuals also utilized coaching.

But of course they do. Professional athletes in every individual sport or athletic discipline—marathoners, triathletes, tennis players, golfers, cyclists, swimmers, etc.—have the support of coaches and others. In fact, one of the things that distinguish the professional athlete from the amateur is the level of coaching support they receive. But amateur athletes, as well, can and do benefit greatly from the help of others who support their goals—coaches, team members, training partners, or simply supportive friends and family members.

When training for my first triathlon, even though I would be competing and crossing the finish line alone, I derived tremendous benefit from the coaches provided by Team In Training, the fundraising arm of the Leukemia and Lymphoma Society, and from the other members of the team with whom I trained. Leveraging the expertise of the coaches and having the support of other team members (as well as my spouse) kept my commitment level high, helped me maintain accountability to the training plan, and ultimately enabled me to achieve my goal of crossing that finish line—with much better performance than I expected.

How this Principle Applies to Your Writing. Writers most often write alone. It is a solitary, and sometimes lonely, task. It is usually accomplished in isolation; there is no one else there telling them what to write. When they complete a book manuscript, it's their achievement alone. But that doesn't mean they did it all by themselves. Read the acknowledgements page of any published book, and you're likely to see the names of many people who had a hand in supporting the author and contributing to her success in completing and publishing the work in some way—spouses, editors, agents, early readers, supportive friends and family members. Writers, like endurance athletes who compete as individuals, have people supporting them. The committed writer recognizes the value of supportive relationships in achieving his goal.

When I was young, I remember reading the acknowledgments page of a book and having much the same reaction I had when I watched that Wimbledon match: I was amazed that the author—who ostensibly wrote the book alone—had so many people supporting him. Like the endurance athlete, the level of commitment a writer has often mirrors his level of support. In fact, it is the level of support a writer has (and cultivates) that distinguishes the committed writer who actually crosses the finish line of a book from one who merely dabbles and does not finish.

I completed a two-year MFA degree program through my own individual efforts; however, it would not have been possible for me to do so without the help of the program's staff, the guidance of my faculty mentors and workshop leaders, and the support of my fellow students and readers who provided invaluable feedback. Similarly, completing this book would not have been possible without the encouragement and guidance of my writing coach, a professional editor (also one of my mentors), and the support of my spouse, among others.

For most writers, writing a book is not a smooth journey from point A to point B. There are fits and starts, setbacks, detours, obstructions, challenges, and unexpected delays. On many days throughout the journey it will seem as if you are taking one step forward and two steps back. If writers, like endurance athletes, were truly alone on the journey, many would not finish and many others would find it far more difficult than it has to be.

Some level of support from people who can, and are willing to, guide you, believe in you, encourage you, inspire you, cheer you on is essential. Such support can come from family members—a spouse or children who understand your need for time to write; a local writing group that meets regularly to read and critique members' work; a writing coach or mentor; or from friends or fellow writers who serve as readers, sounding boards, and trusted sources of constructive feedback.

4. Train mentally as well as physically. The endurance athlete knows that mental conditioning is just as important as physical conditioning. A positive mental state is crucial to optimal physical performance. Observe an athlete performing well and you will observe intensity, focus, concentration, and total immersion in the task at hand. If that focus and concentration is there, that athlete more than likely is going to have a good performance; however, if that focus and concentration is missing, even if it's lost for a moment, performance invariably suffers. Accordingly, mental training is an integral part of the athlete's physical training regimen.

Mental training strategies include positive self-talk, visualization, mentally rehearsing performance, meditation, reframing a negative situation into something more positive, and releasing negative thoughts, emotions, and negative beliefs. Successful athletes incorporate some combination of these strategies into their training program.

Many athletes also develop rituals intended to prepare the mind to enter into a positive mental state just prior to training or competition. All forms of mental training, then, support physical training and performance. And, in turn, physical training supports mental performance. As the athlete enhances conditioning and physical skills, for example, confidence improves, which in turn enhances the mental state. Developing muscle memory—that is, practicing movements over and over to the point where they become second nature, to the point where the body takes over independent of the conscious mind—is also a form of physical training that supports a positive mental state. If an athlete had to consciously think about how to complete each movement it takes to compete, she would be unable to focus in the moment.

This reciprocity of mental energy and physical energy exists because they are both aspects of chi, the life-force energy we talked about in Part 1. Condition the body and as the body's physical plant improves, one's mental environment improves, too. One who feels good physically will also have more mental energy, greater focus and clarity, a better outlook, etc. And one who feels good mentally is also apt to possess more physical energy, to feel better in the body, to move with greater ease, efficiency, and power.

In this heightened state of mental and physical energy, the athlete more easily enters the "flow" state where thought and action (mental and physical energy) align and flow unconsciously and harmoniously. When that happens, hours of intense focus can seem like only minutes. When that happens, effort in the moment seems effortless.

How this Principle Applies to Your Writing. Writing, of course, is primarily a mental activity; very little physical energy is expended during the act of writing; however, creative performance can benefit from proper mental training as much as athletic performance can. Writers can employ many of the same psychological strategies athletes use—including positive self-talk, visualization, meditation, reframing a negative situation into something more positive, and releasing negative thoughts, emotions, and negative beliefs—to improve creative performance and productivity.

And just as the athlete develops pre-training, pre-competition rituals intended to prepare her mind to enter the positive mental state necessary to support athletic performance, the writer, too, can develop rituals—specific thoughts, practices, and mechanical movements or actions—completed just prior to a writing workout that enable the mind to enter a ready-state for producing optimal creative energy. Pre-writing rituals can also be considered analogous to an athlete's physical warm-up exercises that prepare the body for more intense activities to come.

I'll have more to say about pre-writing rituals and how they can help support creative performance in Part 3. For now, consider also that even though very little physical energy is used in the act of handwriting or keyboarding, the reciprocity of mental and physical energy still applies to the writer and can be used to his optimal advantage. As discussed above, those who gain greater physical energy through conditioning the body, also tend to have greater mental, and therefore creative, energy available to them.

Since mental and physical energy are aspects of life-force energy (chi), balancing the two, as the athlete knows, is critical to optimizing the performance of both. For this same reason, it is helpful for the writer, in following the *ChiWriting* program, to incorporate regular physical activity and exercise into daily life, for this will support greater mental (creative) energy at the page.

As I mentioned in the Introduction, it is not necessary for you to use the physical training principles in this book to become an endurance athlete, but you would do well to use them to incorporate about three hours (180 minutes) of focused physical activity over the course of the week — or about thirty to sixty minutes of exercise three to six days a week (depending on how you structure your schedule). Brisk walking, running, swimming, biking, hiking, strength training, calisthenics, aerobics classes, etc., or any combination of these, are good ways to keep your body conditioned in order to maximize the energy available for your creative work and to fulfill your work and family obligations.

5. Recognize the importance of diet and nutrition. The endurance athlete knows that diet and nutrition — the food and water an athlete consumes to fuel his workouts and power his body — are of the utmost importance in proper physical conditioning and improving athletic performance. The body breaks down consumed food to its component parts — glucose, proteins, triglycerides, etc. — and extracts its energy (its chi) to provide power for all bodily processes, as well as building and maintaining muscle, bone, and tissue.

In other words, food and water are the source energy required for the mental and physical energy discussed above. Because of this, whether one is training for a marathon or simply trying to get in better physical shape, it is impossible to out-exercise a bad diet. To borrow a phrase from the computing world: *garbage in, garbage out.* If an athlete fuels her body with garbage — a surplus of junk foods, fried foods, highly refined or processed foods — she cannot expect optimal energy or performance in her daily life, much less optimal athletic performance.

A variety of fresh foods, whole foods, fruits, vegetables, whole grains, lean protein sources, "good" fats, are essential to health, vitality, and physical performance. In fact, nutrition is so important, it probably accounts for at least eighty percent of an athlete's health, well-being, and athletic performance, while physical training and exercise accounts for about twenty percent. Since life-force energy is transferred from the food and water the athlete consumes to her body and mind, the quality of that food and water is fundamental to the health and performance of the body and mind.

In this context, physical and mental training, though highly important, is adjunctive to the need to eat properly and in proportion to the expenditure of energy. No matter how hard an endurance athlete trains, eating a surplus of high-calorie junk food will degrade performance and hamper conditioning.

How this Principle Applies to Your Writing. Remember that one of main premises of *ChiWriting* is that everything is energy and therefore everything is connected. Your body (that is, the condition of your body and how well it functions) is quite literally a product of what you put into it. If you fuel yourself properly, you will be healthier and have more physical energy. If you are healthier and have more physical energy, your creative energy will be enhanced, as well. That is why an effective *ChiWriting* regimen, one that trains and conditions the creative mind, includes the important components of physical exercise and proper nutrition—these are aspects of daily living that must be reengineered to support your writing (more about that in Part 3).

Reading is also essential nutrition for the creative mind. For the writer, it is just as important to fuel the creative mind properly as it is for the endurance athlete to fuel the body properly. Reading is how the creative mind is fed and nourished, which is probably not a surprise to you—writers, and those who want to become writers, naturally tend to read a lot—but if you think about it in terms of the endurance training model we are using here, reading takes on a much more essential role in the life and training of a writer.

Many people eat strictly for enjoyment—the endurance athlete enjoys food too—but the endurance athlete also eats in specific ways for specific purposes: to support physical training, conditioning, and development; all that makes them athletes. Similarly, many people read for enjoyment, as do writers, but the writer also reads in specific ways for specific purposes: to support the training, conditioning, and development of the creative mind in order to create her own books.

As a *ChiWriter*, read widely from a variety of works and genres — fiction, nonfiction, poetry, history, biography, etc. — that align with your goals as a writer. This does not necessarily mean that if you are a fiction writer, you should read only fiction, or that if you are a poet, you should read only poetry. The fiction writer's creative mind can be nourished by the descriptive language in poetry and vice versa. If you are writing a biography, your creative mind could be nourished by the characterizations in a literary novel. If you are writing a memoir, your creative mind could be nourished by the structure of a historical work, and so on.

The key concept here is to read for enjoyment, but not just for enjoyment; read also to instruct and inspire your creative mind, to nourish it so that it's ready to perform well for your writing workouts. I recommend investing at least as much time in reading and you do in writing each week, according to your plan. For example, if your plan calls for six hours of writing workouts per week, you should also read at least six hours per week, a 1:1 ratio at minimum.

I'd also recommend reading with a notebook handy so that you can jot down thoughts and ideas for your own work that come to you as you read — and they will. If you do this, you will find that your writing workouts are much more efficient and productive, just as the endurance athlete's physical workouts are more efficient and productive when the body is properly nourished.

We've now covered ten basic principles that make an endurance athlete successful — that take her from a low energy, out of shape, low-confidence person to one that has transformed her body and conditioned it to cross the finish line of an athletic feat that seemed impossible to her before. We have also seen how these same principles can be adapted to ensure success in your writing life—to take you from a low energy, out of shape, low-confidence person (creatively speaking) to one that conditions your creative mind and supercharges your writing life, enabling you to cross the finish line of your book.

You may have noticed that I am recommending a minimum commitment of fifteen hours weekly toward *ChiWriting* activities: six hours of writing workouts; six hours of reading; and three hours of physical training and exercise. (Supporting these activities by consuming a diet rich in fresh foods—high in life force energy—is also a recommended part of the *ChiWriting* program; however, since you need to eat anyway, there is no real additional time commitment involved.)

At this point, you may be wondering how in the world you are going to fit fifteen hours of additional activities into a schedule already crammed with work commitments, family obligations, and other responsibilities. You may be thinking it's impossible. It's not.

In Part 3, we will cover how to put these principles and strategies into action so that you can meet all of your current obligations and still commit to becoming a *ChiWriter*.

PART 3: BECOMING A *CHIWRITER*

"*Knowing is not enough, we must apply.
Willing is not enough, we must do.*"
— Bruce Lee

"*Take action and insight will follow.*"
— Anne Lamont

In Part 1, we talked about some of the reasons you may find (or have found) it difficult to write a book despite the fact that you have the desire to do so. We discussed the fact that most of these reasons boil down to one thing: your desire to write a book has not yet reached the point at which you are fully willing to face and endure the perceived pain involved in the creative conditioning process (the struggle and hard work, the time investment required, the fear of failure, etc.) so that the pursuit of the goal becomes an autotelic experience; that is, when the perceived pleasure you derive from pursuing the goal overcomes the perceived pain with which you started.

An autotelic activity, you'll recall, is one that is pursued for its intrinsic rewards, irrespective of any external rewards you may or may not receive. When writing becomes an autotelic experience, it doesn't mean the writing won't still be difficult at times, or deeply challenging; it simply means that you derive inner pleasure from the process, despite these difficulties or challenges, and *it's that inner pleasure that drives you.*

Where most people fail is in that gap between the point of commitment—that moment in time in which a decision is made to pursue a goal—and the point at which the activity required to achieve that goal becomes autotelic. Within that gap, tremendous discipline and effort is often required to move through powerful inner resistance. This inner resistance exists despite the desire to achieve a goal and can come in many forms, from simple inertia to the desire to avoid suffering to fear of failure.

It's easy to see here a correlation with physical training. For the conditioned person who exercises regularly, working out is likely an autotelic activity. Despite the challenge of daily training, the conditioned person tends to look forward to, and derive inner pleasure from, the workouts themselves.

For the deconditioned person who wants to get in better shape, however, it's a different story. The deconditioned person is more likely to dread workouts because training is difficult in a deconditioned state; if you want to "get in shape," a certain amount of suffering is required to create that adaptive response over time.

Often, the mere *desire* to become conditioned, in and of itself, does not create the sufficient or sustainable drive necessary to overcome the desire to avoid suffering, so the goal is abandoned. In other words, if inner resistance wins often enough, pursuit of the desired goal is abandoned.

The surest way to reverse this outcome is to make the choice daily, hard as it may be in the beginning, to keep going despite inner resistance. Over time, as these daily choices are made, new habits supporting the goal are formed. The tremendous discipline and effort required to overcome inner resistance lessens as physical and mental energy systems adapt to the effort, conditioning gains are realized, and autotelic momentum begins to take over.

At that point, though the workouts may still be difficult and challenging, inner resistance is replaced with inner satisfaction. The athlete may even begin to enter into a flow state, that "sweet spot" of experience in which the effortful seems effortless. At that point, achievement of the goal is far more likely, if not assured.

The process of creative conditioning is much the same. Creative conditioning, like physical conditioning, occurs over time in response to specific stimuli. In the beginning, following the point of commitment, inner resistance must be overcome through daily choice, disciplined effort, and new habit formation. As conditioning improves, however, the effort involved becomes less effortful; you are driven not by the sheer discipline it takes to overcome inner resistance but by the inner satisfaction derived from the effort.

At that point, you are much more likely to continue the training necessary to reach the goal. Like the endurance athlete who physically trains, you will also begin to enter into a state of flow during writing sessions: full immersion and total focus in the job at hand so that the energy involved seems at times to flow effortlessly, even joyfully. Of course, as any endurance athlete will tell you, you will have days when this flow is stronger than others, but the longer you continue to train, the more often you will be likely to experience these stronger days.

In Part 2, we discussed the use of endurance training principles as a model for maintaining consistent focus on the thoughts and actions necessary to follow through on your commitment to write a book. You now know the three basic workouts every endurance athlete uses to progressively condition her body and how those same workouts can be applied to the writing process to progressively condition your creative mind. You also know the planning and training principles endurance athletes use to structure a focused training program over a "season" (a period of months), or even multiple seasons if necessary, that leads to crossing the finish line in a signature event; and, you know how those same principles can be applied toward structuring a writing program that can lead you across the finish line of your book.

Of course, simply knowing this information is not enough. You must take action to apply this knowledge and you must take action consistently over time until your goal is achieved—especially within that gap where most people fail (i.e., between the point of commitment and the point of conditioning where autotelic satisfaction begins to drive the action).

Part 3 is about how to do this. In this final section, we will explore specific ways you can shift your mindset and daily actions to fully support your writing goal. We will look at a practical and systematic approach you can take to optimize your physical and mental energy and how you can harness that energy by developing a thorough training plan for your writing using the principles already discussed. And, finally we will cover tips and strategies for staying focused and on track with your plan.

"Minding" the Gap

If you are reading this book, you want to write a book; you may already have made the decision to write one. That decision is your point of commitment. We talked about the point of commitment as that moment in time in which your choice causes your life's wave function superposition to collapse to a definite future state—that of being a book writer. Of all the infinite future life possibilities available to you, you have chosen to be a book writer.

Remember the metaphor of the rowboat in the middle of the ocean? You are in that rowboat and before you stretches a vast horizon with an infinite number of ports. You set your sights on a single port and make a commitment to reach it. Having passed that point of commitment, having made that definite choice, you now need to maintain consistent focus on the proper thought and action (mental and physical chi) necessary to reach that port, to manifest your choice, to bring it to reality.

Part 3: Becoming a ChiWriter

There is tremendous power in that point of commitment. It is absolutely necessary. Once that commitment is made, the journey, the mental and physical effort must begin. But there is also that gap to contend with.

The truth is, most of us, when we make a commitment to achieve a goal, are incapable of reaching that goal at the outset. At the beginning of the journey, we simply do not have the physical and mental capacity necessary to reach the end of the journey. That comes over time as we learn and grow and adapt. As conditioning gains are made, our capabilities naturally increase; as capabilities increase, we begin to reach a state of autotelic momentum where we derive inner satisfaction from the effort—then, we know with increasing confidence that we are capable, that we will reach our goal.

But making that kind of progress is difficult. It requires new actions, new habits, and that entails a certain amount of suffering. That is why, in that gap between the point of commitment and the point at which autotelic momentum begins to drive our efforts, many give up the pursuit.

While struggling against the ocean currents in your rowboat to reach your chosen port, seemingly far away, you glimpse from the corner of your eye another port that looks much closer, more inviting, easier to reach because the currents—your existing habits and patterns of living—are flowing that way. And so you stop rowing before you reach the point of autotelic momentum.

This happens because most people either underestimate the difficulty of bridging that gap or overestimate their ability to do so. When they underestimate the difficulty, it is easy to fall back into existing habits and patterns of living that do not support the goal. When they overestimate their ability, they become frustrated when results do not come quickly enough and so they give up, thinking it's too much work, not worth it. Even worse, they may view themselves as failures, so what's the use of continuing?

The ability to achieve any goal often comes down to how effective one is in "minding" the gap between the point of commitment and the point at which conditioning gains induce the autotelic rewards necessary to carry on. Within this gap, you must create new daily action habits that support commitment to the process that will lead to the achievement of your goal.

But how do you do that, especially in light of all your existing responsibilities? After all, you no doubt already have habits in place and an existing structure to your days (probably largely imposed on you by external demands, such as work schedules, children's schedules, etc.) and the thought of adding another large commitment (like writing a book) is stress-inducing, to say the least. How do you adapt *ChiWriting* tools and principles we talked about in Part 2 to your particular circumstances so that the process you create and the habits you develop work for you?

Let's first look at how we are traditionally taught to create new habits. When we want to create a new habit that supports some goal, the normal course of action is to focus consciously on completing the desired action every day, perhaps at a set time, and, once the action has been consciously completed over a period of days or weeks, the action will then become a habit, or we will complete the action without too much thought or stress because it has become "normal" for us to do so. We might also combine this practice with traditional time management techniques designed to "save" us time or carve out a silo of time needed to perform the action that will lead to the new habit.

For example, we might say to ourselves: "I am going to cut out one hour of television in the evening and go to bed one hour earlier and get up one hour earlier so that I can write. This might be difficult at first, but if I persevere, I will create a new habit of doing this and then it will no longer be difficult, it will become easy to do."

This is simple enough, and necessary, and effective if sustained over time. Why then do so many fail at maintaining new habits after making a commitment? Why is it so easy to give up in that gap and make a self-defeating choice to fall back into old patterns?

I'm convinced that the reason most people fail at accomplishing any major goal—whether it's getting in shape or writing a book or something else—is that they tend to see the goal, and therefore the new habits necessary to achieve it, in isolation. They set out to accomplish something, but without comprehending the effects that working toward the goal will have on the rest of their lives.

Most would-be writers approach their goal in this way. They may say to themselves, "I'm going to write for an hour a day." They begin with all good intentions, but then what happens after a few days, or a few weeks, is that old habits and old patterns of living reassert themselves and squelch their efforts. They may change that one thing in that one period of time during their day, but the rest of the day, their normal patterns take over and eventually lead them right back to where they were before.

What is happening is that while they are attempting to establish new habits to support commitment to their goal, the attempt to establish these new habits itself goes unsupported. To overcome this tendency, the new action habits necessary to achieve your goal must be supported by new habits of mind. This is what I mean by "minding" the gap. I put "minding" in quotes because success in bridging the gap depends upon your mind, your thinking, your mental approach, the mental energy behind your physical efforts.

Three Habits of Mind

Perhaps you have tried the traditional approach to new habit formation and time management as described above in the past and failed. Instead of that approach—instead of trying to carve out an hour a day of "siloed" time to write—what if you took a more holistic approach? What if you first overhauled your mindset and lifestyle so that the goal of writing your book was approached in a holistic way that was integrated into daily life; in a fundamental way in which the energy ("chi") of mind and body was supported and served as a foundation for growth, so that not only that one hour a day was helping you achieve your goal, but the other twenty-three hours of the day were as well?

If you want to achieve a big goal, you can't do it with a siloed approach; the whole of your life energy must support your goal. Remember, everything is connected, so we must address the structural issues, the existing patterns in our lives, that make it easy to veer back into old routines that do not support the habits we want to create. This requires new habits of mind—a fundamental mental paradigm shift.

Here again, the writer can model the endurance athlete. Most successful endurance athletes display three interrelated habits of mind that are key to supporting their success and ability to maintain consistent action and focus on their goals over time:

1. Integrate, don't add.
2. Stay "in training."
3. Manage energy, not just time.

As a writer, you can use these same habits of mind to create new ways of thinking about your writing goals that support the consistent actions and focus necessary to achieve them. Let's look at each one.

1. Integrate, don't add. The first key habit of mind is a paradigm shift away from "adding-on" and toward "integration." You must not view the planning, actions, habits, and behaviors necessary to achieve your writing goal as "add-ons," as simply additional demands that must be met on top of all your other existing life responsibilities. Instead, they must be integrated seamlessly into your life.

ChiWriting is a set of tools and strategies through which a highly individualized and structured process is created for writing your book. But its structure can't be superimposed upon the structure that already exists in your life for meeting all your other responsibilities. That would make it creaky, unstable, and liable to crash down at any moment. Rather, by *integrating ChiWriting* principles into your existing life structure you strengthen and stabilize the overall structure and consistent forward progress toward your goals and responsibilities in every life domain—work, family, self-care, *and* writing—is supported.

To understand what I mean, imagine two silos standing together, one is "Work," and the other is "Life." Into the work silo are piled all the goals, tasks, obligations, and responsibilities associated with making a living and paying the bills. Into the life silo is crammed everything else: attending to the needs and responsibilities involving your spouse/partner, children, extended family, friends, as well as maintaining some semblance of self-care: eating, sleeping, exercising, leisure, recreation, etcetera. Most people tend to keep these two silos separate and try somehow to keep them in balance as much as possible. But the struggle with this "work/life balance" becomes an obligation in itself and another source of stress and frustration.

The two-silo metaphor helps to visually illustrate the structural paradigm most of us live within every day: For many people, the work silo sucks up most of the time, energy, and attention while the life silo frequently ends up getting short shrift (particularly in regard to self-care). It is into this paradigm that most people try to squeeze in yet another silo for the life goals that are important to them, such as (for our purposes) writing a book. And it helps explain why it's so difficult to successfully manage such an undertaking and accomplish that goal. In meeting the demands of the work silo, we struggle to keep up with the demands of the life silo; how in the world, then, are we supposed to fit in a third silo?

"Work/life balance" is a popular term most of us are familiar with; and because it's familiar we tend to assume it has validity, and that therefore we should strive to achieve it. But in reality, there is no such thing as "work/life balance" because there is no such thing as "work" separate from "life" or "life" separate from "work." In reality, *it's all life*.

And what is life? Life is energy and energy connects all things, unifies all things, as we discussed in Part 1. The two-silo work/life paradigm reinforces a false sense of separateness in which balancing the two becomes a zero-sum game—one silo's gain is the other silo's loss—and the chief currency is time. Once time is spent in one silo, it cannot be regained in the other; and, as mentioned earlier, it is often the life silo that loses out.

Here is where it is necessary to shift your mindset and reframe the situation. Instead of trying to find a "balance" between separate work/life silos—a separation that doesn't really exist—view your life as "desiloed" and begin to see that the important goals in each of your life domains are not segregated and in competition with each other, but rather integrated and supportive of each other.

In this desiloed model, every aspect of life and of daily living is seen as integral to the training necessary to complete the writing goal. In other words, the writing goal and the actions required to meet that goal must be integrated into the writer's life, and not be viewed as separate, as an "add-on."

This is where many writers stumble. They want to write more; they want to complete a book, but if they view it as adding one more thing to do in an already busy life, it becomes easy to avoid it, to simply cut it out, when time is short or when stress enters the picture in the form of other life demands. You will tell yourself you can simply add it back on later, but more often than not, that doesn't happen. The better option is to integrate it into your life in such a way that everything you do is connected to the goal of completing your book.

The second key habit of mind can help you do this.

2. Stay "in training." Once you move to a desiloed model of living — a habit of mind in which your goals in every life domain are integrated and supportive of one another, it becomes a matter of making the right choices that support your goals. A habit of mind that enables you to make the right choices consistently is to do what the endurance athlete does and stay "in training." When athletes begin the process of conditioning and preparing themselves to compete in an event or a series of events, they are said to be "in training."

Now, in the work world, "training" has a different connotation that it does in the athletic world. In the work world, when you are in training, you are learning a new job or a new process so that, upon completion of the training, you become qualified to perform that job or process. By asking you to adopt a habit of mind that you are "in training" as a writer, I do not mean to imply that you are a neophyte who knows nothing about writing and therefore needs to undergo special training for a period of time after which you will be qualified as a "writer."

I mean it in the sense that athletes, even professional athletes, use the term. When athletes are "in training" they do not use the term solely to describe the time specifically invested in physical training to condition their bodies for competition; rather, it describes the totality of the time period — weeks, months, or even years — spent preparing for a signature event. They are consciously working a twenty-four/seven process over a period of time (typically a "season") that will culminate in the completion of their athletic goals — winning a game, a race, or some other type of athletic competition, be it team-focused or an individual performance.

Let's use an example from the world of endurance training to illustrate. Michael Phelps, twenty-three-time Olympic Gold medalist in swimming—an event that requires a tremendous level of conditioning and endurance—was "in training" during an extended period of time each year to prepare for every one of his races. His daily "workouts" consisted of six hours or more in the pool, swimming lap after lap, practicing his strokes and pushing himself.

But his daily workouts were only one component of his training. Every one of the remaining eighteen hours in his day was also focused on a necessary component of his training: When he slept and rested, he was allowing his body to repair itself and recover from his workouts—an extremely important part of the athletic conditioning process. When he ate, it was to give his body the calories and optimal nutrients necessary to fuel his body properly. When he relaxed by reading or listening to music, or watching TV, or spending time with his family, it was to refresh his mind and body so that he could return to his workouts fully focused and reenergized.

When I say I want you to consider yourself "in training," I mean I want you to think about completing your book in the same terms. When you make the conscious commitment to achieve the goal of writing a book, you begin a training period during which everything you do is focused on achieving your goal of completing your book—and I do mean everything.

Let's say you set aside one hour per day to write. You are not "in training" for only that one hour per day. That is only your "workout" period—the time devoted to actually committing words to the page. When you adopt the habit of mind that you are "in training" as a writer, every other hour of your day is also focused on supporting both that daily "workout" time and your overall goal:

- The time you invest sleeping is just as important because your body needs rest if it is to maintain its energy.

- The time you invest eating, and the type of food you choose to eat, is important also for fueling your body and maintaining the physical and mental energy levels necessary to pursue your goals.

- The time you invest at your job is part of your training because it allows you to maintain a lifestyle that enables you to write.

- The time you invest with family, or relaxing, or in other forms of self-care is important because these activities refresh your body and mind so that you can return to your daily writing "workouts" renewed and reenergized.

Notice that I used the term "invest," not "spend" when speaking of time here. This is an important distinction when it comes to supporting these habits of mind. When you "spend" money there is typically little or no return involved, or the return is short-term and fleeting; when you "invest," however, you expect a long-term return on your investment—you expect to get back more than what you put in. The same is true of time.

When you make choices about what you will do during your days and weeks from the perspective of these habits of mind—integrate, don't add and stay "in training"—you are investing time rather than spending it because you get a long-term return on your investment: greater energy, greater productivity, greater likelihood of achieving your goals.

Every day, throughout your day, you are making choices that support your writing goals in some way, shape, or form. Twenty-four/seven, you have the habit of mind as a writer that you are "in training" even though you may not be actually at the page putting down words—just as the athlete is continually "in training" even though she may not be actually physically working out.

This habit of mind helps integrate the goal of completing your book into your life so that the necessary work and action habits is not pushed aside or crowded out by the other life priorities, which are always there. Instead, your other life priorities support and enhance your goal. It also enables maximum flexibility for those times when other life priorities invariably do take precedence.

Let's say an important project deadline at work requires a few late nights, or a sick child needs to be taken care of. Both these occurrences, and myriad others like them in your life, may cut into or interrupt your daily writing workout—and they obviously must be dealt with. But with the mindset that you remain always "in training," your overall writing goal will not suffer appreciably in the long term if you simply and calmly make the necessary adjustments and continue on with your training plan.

If, for example, a planned sixty-minute tempo writing workout is interrupted by the need to attend to a sick child, you complete a ten-minute or twenty-minute high intensity writing workout instead. Or instead of your planned two-a-day writing workouts, you complete just one until an urgent work project is complete. When life happens, as it always does, you adjust the training and continue on, you don't just abandon the goal.

Can you see how these two habits of mind are interrelated and essential, especially if you lead a busy life and don't have much time to spare?

Adopting the mindset of staying "in training" twenty-four/seven enables you to integrate the goal of writing a book into your life, not simply add it onto an already busy life; integrating the goal into your life enables you to stay in training, so that every choice you make about how to invest your time supports your goals. The third habit of mind is similarly interrelated and mutually supportive.

3. Manage energy, not just time. Because it's all life and all life is energy, when we shift to a desiloed pattern of living—characterized by the habits of mind in which our writing goals are integrated with goals in other life domains and we stay "in training" to achieve them—we move from time-based currency, which is spent, to energy-based capital, which is invested.

We don't focus solely on managing time and then "spending" appropriate amounts of time in separate silos; we focus primarily on managing energy and "investing" appropriate amounts of energy on the goals and responsibilities most important to us—an investment that pays off with greater productivity and progress toward our goals.

Probably one of the main reasons you haven't written your book yet is that you have demanding work and family responsibilities that require most of your time and energy. You get up in the morning, deal with family and household responsibilities, get yourself ready for work, perhaps endure a long commute to your office or workplace where you put in grueling hours, only to come home to face more family and household responsibilities. After you take care of those, maybe you plop on the couch exhausted to get a couple hours of relaxation by watching television before you fall into bed so you can get a few hours sleep before starting all over again.

With a schedule like that, how on earth are you ever going to find time to write your book? There's just no time—no extra time—in your day to get it done. To that, I say, you are right. There is no extra time in the day. Everyone has the same twenty-four hours per day so you are not going to "find" extra time. Sure, there are plenty of books and strategies that can help with time management, with organizing your day according to certain principles that enable you to manage your time more efficiently. That can be effective to an extent. But even if you are able to manage your time more efficiently to create "extra" time in your daily schedule, the question becomes: will you have the energy to properly utilize that extra time to move toward your goal?

The better strategy is to stop focusing strictly on managing your time and instead focus on managing your energy. You cannot add more time to your day, but you *can* enhance and optimize your energy. You don't "need" extra time because there is no such thing, but there is always energy because there is an unlimited supply of energy—that's all anything is, energy, including you.

Energy is always available to you and you absolutely can harvest more of it through proper diet/nutrition, exercise, and sleep. Once you harvest more energy, you can then make more conscious choices about how you invest that energy. So the key to accomplishing your writing goals in the face of demanding responsibilities in other areas of your life is not time management, per se, but energy and choice management. Once you draw more energy into your life and make good decisions about where to invest that energy, you will be amazed how much more "time" you seem to have to accomplish your writing goals.

To sum up: it's important to integrate a big goal like writing a book into your life, not simply view it as an "add-on," as one additional responsibility on top of everything else you have to do. To integrate this goal into your life, it's essential to adopt the mindset that you are always "in training." The endurance athlete is not in training only when she is actually working out; she is in training twenty-four/seven because everything else she does supports the time and energy invested in working out. Similarly, the writer is not "in training" only when he is actually at the page; he is in training twenty-four/seven because everything he does supports the time invested in writing. Finally, staying "in training" means managing not just time but energy—life energy, chi, the fundamental basis for all of life and everything we do or experience.

Like life itself, the foundation for the habits of mind and the habits of action necessary to achieve your goals is chi—life energy. Without adequate stores of life energy, not much is accomplished in any life arena.

It begins with energizing.

Energizing: The Components of Chi

Remember that the basis of this book and its approach to writing is that energy is everything. Energy—chi—is really all there is. As you read this, energy (chi) is coursing through your body and mind, powering your physiological systems—respiration, circulation, digestion, temperature regulation, sensation, motor movement—all of these systems are energized without your conscious thought, each of the trillions of cells in your body its own tiny factory pumping out energy in accordance with its specific function.

Energy is also powering your thought processes, which are physically characterized by electrical and chemical impulses in the brain but which are also the product of the more mysterious mind. Your mind, in the physical form of your brain's electrical and chemical impulses, is automatically processing these words as you read them, translating them into an understanding of the ideas, concepts, and meanings they are intended to convey. And all of this—both physiological and thought processes—is made possible by your body's continuous interaction with the energetic matrix surrounding you at all times—the physical and mental matrices discussed in Part 1.

Chi operates through the physical environment: you derive energy from the oxygen you breathe, the fluids you drink, the foods you eat, the movements you make, and the rest you take. But chi also operates through a mental environment—as thought that directs our actions; as imagination that explores possibilities; as knowledge that expands our understanding of the world; and, as emotions that enliven and deepen our experience.

Chi is always flowing but it can also be stored. Remember that Einstein proved the equivalency of matter and energy—matter is really energy stored in a certain form. In the earth, tremendous amounts of energy are stored as the natural gas and oil that fuel our homes, our planes, trains, and automobiles, our factories. In the body, energy is stored as glycogen in the liver and muscles and as fat in adipose tissue—when we take in more energy than we expend, our fat stores expand to hold that excess energy. When we expend more energy than we take in, the body utilizes its stored energy for fuel.

As writers, we store creative energy on the page that is then transformed into an experience for the reader. The poet Robert Frost said, "No tears in the writer, no tears in the reader. No surprise in the writer, no surprise in the reader."

He was describing an energetic relationship between the writer and the reader. When you write, you transcribe the creative energy of your imagination, storing this chi on the page (whether ink on paper, or pixels on a screen) in the form of strange symbols we know as letters, arranged in specific configurations known as words, and then strung together as sentences and paragraphs that convey a thought, an idea, an image, an experience. When these words are picked up by readers through our shared knowledge of language and word meanings, the creative energy the writer stored there is reconstituted as thought energy in the reader, and as a result the reader is changed—the reader is educated, informed, enlightened, entertained; the reader is moved in some way that expands her experience.

Isn't it thrilling to realize that when we read a poem by Frost we are experiencing, in our own way, the feelings and emotions he experienced when writing it? That when we identify with what a character in a story or novel or memoir is going through, we are recognizing and experiencing that character's feelings and emotions through the creative energy the writer developed and stored on the page for that very purpose?

And it doesn't matter how long ago a book was written—years, decades, centuries—when a reader picks up a book written long ago and is stirred by its words, that energy is as vital as it was when the writer first felt it. It's as if the writer's words strike a tuning fork and that vibration causes musical strings deep within us to resonate with that same note, that same frequency.

In a very real sense, the energetic relationship between writer and reader—the writer's chi stored there on the page that flows again when accessed and experienced by the reader—is timeless, and is indicative of the timeless nature of energy—of life—itself.

Since everything is energy, including the creative work we writers store on the page, it makes sense to pay attention to the channels of energy in our lives, to the ways in which we interact with and access energy from the energetic matrix of which we are an integral part.

This is how, as a *ChiWriter*, you will manage energy, rather than simply time, to focus on your book.

When we "energize" properly, we enhance both our physical and creative conditioning, which means we enhance both our ability to effectively integrate our writing goals into the structure of our lives, and our ability to creatively execute our writing.

There are essentially five components of chi—five ways we access and process life energy: through *breathing, drinking, eating,* and *moving,* and also through *rest,* both physical and mental. All of these are fundamental to our very existence, so fundamental that most of us don't think about them much.

We breathe without thinking because it's autonomic; we drink and eat as a matter of course throughout the day because we must. Often, though, we drink and eat purely for pleasure, or simply to stave off thirst and hunger with whatever is handy, not in a conscious way that supports our bodies' needs. We move to get from place to place, but often not with conscious effort to strengthen and enhance physical conditioning. And physical and mental rest often takes the form of simply falling into bed at night exhausted and getting a few hours of fitful sleep before we start all over again.

Properly energizing for the purposes of becoming a *ChiWriter* and achieving your writing goals means accessing and managing energy through each of these channels in a more conscious and proactive way in order to cultivate and enhance our physical, mental, and creative energy. Let's look at each one to see how this can be accomplished.

Breathing. Most people don't breathe properly. It may seem silly to say this because it's such an autonomic response. We breathe automatically, without conscious thought, so how can we be doing it improperly? The reason is that many of us are physically deconditioned. Many of us lead such inactive, sedentary lives that there is no need to breathe properly, which is to say fully and deeply. Rather, we tend to take short, shallow breaths that don't fully expand our lungs.

Over time, this becomes our "normal" way of breathing. The capability of the autonomic response is diminished, the muscles and organs involved in breathing — the diaphragm and lungs — are weakened. In this weakened state, the blood is not delivering as much oxygen to the cells of our bodies, or is doing so inefficiently, and as a result cell function is diminished. We feel tired, fatigued, sluggish. And since brain cells, like other cells of the body, are not being properly nourished with oxygen, mental processes also suffer. We feel mentally tired, unable to focus, anxious, stressed out.

Regular deep breathing is the antidote. This is accomplished through conditioning the body to increase aerobic capacity through exercise. A person who is aerobically conditioned — who regularly pushes her anaerobic threshold up through physical training, as we talked about in Part 2—naturally breathes more fully and deeply than someone who is physically deconditioned. This is why a person who is physically conditioned has more energy, feels more energetic both physically and mentally.

The conditioned person is better able to meet the physical demands of daily living, and naturally feels more mentally alert and focused, as well. So exercise and physical training are an essential part of the equation, as we will discuss further soon. But there is also another way to enhance breathing and the energetic benefits it offers and that is to make a conscious effort several times a day to breathe deeply and focus on your breath.

Take a minute or two at regular intervals throughout your day to consciously breathe—before each meal, snack, or coffee break, for example; or, set up reminders on your smartphone. Breathe slowly and deeply. Inhale slowly, concentrating on the breath flowing up your nostrils into your body, nourishing every cell with oxygen. And then exhale slowly, concentrating on the outflow of breath, releasing from the body that which it no longer needs.

Do this rhythmically: Inhale slowly through the nose for a count of four, drawing oxygen deeply in, expanding the belly. Hold for a count of two, then exhale slowly through the mouth for a count of four. Be conscious of the vivifying process of breath; feel the circulating loop of inflowing/outflowing energy exchange with your environment and your essential place within it. Wherever you are and whatever you are doing at any given moment, you are an integral part of an energetic, life-sustaining environmental matrix.

Drinking. Hydration is as important to the body and brain as breathing. Just as your cells need oxygen, they also need water to properly carry out their physiological functions. A state of dehydration has the same ill effects on physical and mental processes as short, shallow, inefficient breathing.

If you are dehydrated, you will feel tired, fatigued, and sluggish. Mentally, you are more likely to feel anxious, stressed out, unable to focus. An endurance athlete who is not properly hydrated—or who does not maintain proper electrolyte balance or glucose levels—during an event will quickly find her body shutting down. Electrolytes are minerals (such as sodium, potassium, magnesium, etc.) that conduct electrical charges in cells. When electrolytes are lost in sweat, they must be replaced for cells to continue functioning properly.

Similarly, glucose, which the body "burns" for energy, must be replaced during extended periods of exertion. This is why, in addition to water, endurance athletes consume sports drinks, gels, or other forms of easily digestible nutrition during long events.

For purposes of "energizing" to become a *ChiWriter*, you do not need to consume extra amounts of electrolytes or glucose—this is typically only necessary for periods of sustained physical exertion lasting more than two or three hours. Still, it is always important to maintain proper hydration during normal daily activities, even those that don't involve a lot of exertion.

Many people, however, do not consciously consume pure water throughout the day in order to maintain optimal hydration. Instead, they drink other fluids, such as coffee, milk, soda, juices, alcohol, etc., and the body derives whatever water it can from these fluids and from the foods eaten (since solid foods also contain certain amounts of water).

If this is the route you are compelling your body to take, you may or may not be getting adequate amounts of water. It depends on the water content of the foods you eat, and the amount of fluids you drink—some fluids, particularly coffee, caffeinated sodas, and alcohol, are diuretic, meaning they promote water loss through urination. If you drink a six-ounce cup of coffee, for example, you are not getting the hydrating benefits of the six ounces of water in that coffee, you are getting something less than that since coffee promotes urination.

Conventional wisdom says you should drink eight, eight-ounce cups of water throughout the day in addition to the other fluids and foods you consume. But most people find this difficult to do and, again, depending on the amount of other types of fluids you drink and the water content of the foods you eat, this may be unnecessary, or even too much for some people.

The best course of action to ensure that you maintain the proper hydration necessary for optimal physical and mental functioning is to consciously consume pure water at regular points throughout the day. My own personal regimen is to consume one cup of water: immediately upon waking; before, during, and after exercising; around mid-afternoon; and then mid-evening before bedtime. This means that on most days, I consume five or six cups of water in addition to the water content in the other fluids and foods I consume.

If you do not currently drink water at regular intervals in addition to the other fluids and foods you consume, I recommend you do so and experiment to see what works best for you. You may, for example, prefer to drink a cup of water upon waking, during exercise, and before every meal. Or, you may find it's easier to fill a large bottle with water and sip it throughout the day. Whatever works for you; the key is to stay well-hydrated—your urine should be clear to pale yellow in color—and, importantly, to drink *consciously*, that is, to be mindful of the purpose and intent in consuming water.

Like the one- or two-minute breaks you will take several times a day to breathe fully and rhythmically, drawing oxygen deeply into your body, pausing for water breaks throughout the day will serve as anchor points for consciously connecting to source energy.

When you drink, savor the feel and taste of the water in your mouth. When you swallow, experience the refreshing, cool feeling as the water glides down your throat into your belly. Visualize the water's life-sustaining energy spreading to every cell in your body. This will help you stay not only well-hydrated, but well-energized throughout the day.

Eating. Like breathing and drinking, eating involves a complex process of energy extraction and delivery that we don't consciously control (aside from what we choose to eat). From breathing air, your body extracts and delivers energy in the form of oxygen. From drinking fluids, your body extracts and delivers energy in the form of water. From eating foods, your body extracts and delivers energy in the form of carbohydrates, protein, and fat.

These macronutrients perform vital functions in the body and also deliver essential micronutrients—vitamins and minerals. Carbohydrates provide glucose, which fuels the body, and fiber, which aids in digestion and elimination. Protein provides amino acids, which build and maintain muscle and tissue, and also enzymes that support cell function in many ways. Fat delivers essential fatty acids that are necessary structural components of cells and aid in micronutrient absorption. Stored fat also provides a ready source of fuel for the body.

Food is also delicious. It tastes good. Beyond its purely physiological functions, food delivers emotional benefits. Eating delicious food provides immense pleasure and satisfaction. It *feels* good to eat. It can be comforting. Eating is also social and even celebratory; sharing a meal is a way to enhance and enliven connections to family and friends.

Many of us tend to focus solely on these pleasurable aspects of food and eating—to our detriment, because by focusing on the emotional benefits of eating we tend to make food choices based solely on taste, convenience, and pleasure, not on the nutritional aspects so vital to the body. The result is that overall health and energy suffer.

The modern processed, packaged food industry and the fast food restaurant industry have largely engineered this result by loading their products with copious amounts of salt, sugar, and fat—elements that make food delicious and light up pleasure centers in the brain, making us eat lots and crave more—while treating nutritional content as an afterthought.

When you eat lots of overly processed foods, fast foods, and junk foods—foods high in calories but low in energy and nutritional content—your body uses all the same processes as when you eat good, fresh, whole, nutritious food: you chew and swallow and your body's digestive system goes into action like it always does to extract the nutrients and energy in that food, except that there's very little nutritional content and energy to extract and the end result is your body—bones, muscle, tissue, cells—is not properly nourished, while the excess, empty calories consumed are stored as fat.

The predictable outcome is a body that is overfed but undernourished, a body in poor health, ultimately ill-equipped to carry out its normal energetic functions. This is why, in terms of overall population health, we suffer from high rates of obesity, illness, and chronic, debilitating, diet-related conditions, such as Type II diabetes and heart disease.

If you find yourself in this nutritional boat—primarily eating foods high in calories but low in energy and nutritional content—you probably feel tired and sluggish much of the time. You may struggle to accomplish all of your many normal daily responsibilities and may easily become stressed or feel overwhelmed. If you feel stressed or overwhelmed, you are far more likely to eat even more tasty but unhealthy foods in order to derive compensating pleasure and emotional benefits. But of course the pleasure derived is fleeting and will only perpetuate long-term ill effects on health and energy.

In such a negative nutritional state, it's easy to feel as if there's not enough *time* in the day to accomplish everything you want to accomplish—including writing your book. Actually though, you're probably not suffering from a time deficit as much as an energy deficit. If this energy deficit were replaced with an energy surplus, you would likely enjoy far greater productivity and accomplish much more, even though the same amount of time is available to you.

The vast majority of endurance athletes invest substantial time physically training in addition to other significant work and family responsibilities. They are able to do this not because they have more time, but because they have more energy. They have more energy, in part, because they view food primarily as a source of fuel rather than simply a source of momentary tasty pleasure.

The endurance athlete knows that in order to accomplish her athletic goals, she must fuel her body properly, with nutrient-dense foods that provide the right energetic balance of carbohydrates, protein, and fat to support her physical training. This does not mean the endurance athlete doesn't enjoy food, derive pleasure from eating, or can't indulge—or even overindulge—now and then.

But it does mean that, most of the time, she makes mindful choices about how she fuels her body. She knows that to achieve quality energy output, she must choose quality energy input. And because her body is in better physical condition, it naturally craves foods that are more nutritionally dense, therefore it is easier for her to make better food choices *and* eating those better foods becomes more pleasurable.

As a *ChiWriter*, you can begin to derive greater benefits from eating by viewing food in the same way the endurance athlete does: not as a source of momentary pleasure, primarily, but as a source of fuel to energize and power you toward your goals. Remember that since everything is connected, physical and mental energy—different manifestations of the same life force—are synergistic in nature, each supporting the other. Choosing better quality energy input by consuming nutrient-dense foods most of the time will ensure better quality energy output both physically and mentally, resulting in greater and more productive creative progress.

There is no shortage of information available about how to eat better. Thousands of books, magazines, articles, diet programs, and related products are devoted to diet, food, and nutrition, with thousands more added each year (counteracting the detrimental health effects of a modern diet driven by billion-dollar industries in processed, packaged junk foods has itself become a billion-dollar industry). The problem is how to make sense of all the information out there—some of it good, but much of it conflicting, gimmicky, and plain ineffective, or even harmful.

Fortunately, for the purposes of eating to fuel and energize the body properly, *ChiWriters* (and endurance athletes) really only need to remember seven words:

"Eat food. Not too much. Mostly plants."

These seven words were written by author Michael Pollan in his book, "In Defense of Food: An Eater's Manifesto." They are powerful and profound in their simplicity. With just seven words expressing three simple concepts, Pollan successfully encapsulates all we know about proper nutrition and healthy eating. Use them as guideposts for daily diet choices that will ensure your body and mind are properly nourished and energized for your creative work. To elaborate a bit more, here is my own take on what they mean:

"Eat food" means to eat *real* food, food that is whole and fresh, as close as possible to its natural state: whole grains, fruits, vegetables, nuts, legumes are good sources of quality complex carbohydrates and fiber, while fresh dairy, eggs, and meats—beef, chicken, pork, seafood—are good sources of protein and fat. Some vegetable sources are also good sources of protein: soy, quinoa, and beans, for example.

Fresh, whole foods are nutrient-dense; they are high in chi, or life-force energy. Remember that the same life-force that powers your body and mind also powers the plants and animal products you consume as food. When you consume these foods in as fresh and whole a form as possible, most of that life-force energy is still present and available to be extracted and delivered to the cells of your body.

Foods that are heavily processed or refined, including many packaged foods, fast foods, fried foods, and sugary foods, are high in calories—mostly from sugar and fat—but low in life-force energy and therefore low in the nutrients your body needs to fuel itself. It's best to view these types of foods as "treats," not as primary components of your daily diet. Eat real food most of the time and "treat" food only occasionally.

"Not too much" means to be mindful of how much you consume so as not to overeat. Many people who eat a diet lacking in fresh, whole foods actually overeat significantly because high amounts of sugar, fat, and salt in the foods they tend to consume—processed, fried, fast, junk—make those foods taste so good. Not only do these foods taste yummy, which encourages overeating, they prime the brain to crave more of these types of food, almost like an addiction.

If you eat until you feel stuffed, that is a good indication that you've taken in more calories than your body needs. Any excess calories, of course, will be stored as fat. This is true no matter what type of food you eat. Even if your diet is rich in fresh, whole foods high in nutritive value, eating too much of it will result in excess calories being stored as fat in the body. A good rule of thumb, therefore, is to eat slowly and mindfully, really enjoying your food, and then stop at the point you feel satisfied, not at the point you feel stuffed.

"Mostly plants" means to center your diet primarily around plant-based foods, rather than animal-based foods. Many people eat a meat-centered diet, building meals around a traditional "meat and potatoes" model, with an emphasis on the meat. Fresh fruits and vegetables, if they are eaten at all, are often treated as an afterthought.

Meat and other animal-based products deliver high-quality protein the body needs, but they can also deliver high levels of fat and are deficient in the fiber and many micronutrients provided by plant-based foods. The overconsumption of meat in meat-centered diets can therefore lead to a host of issues that can negatively impact health and energy.

When planning your daily diet, a good strategy is to make sure one-half to three-quarters of your meals and snacks consist of whole plant-based foods.

By adhering to these three simple dietary concepts most of the time, your diet will naturally be comprised primarily of foods that are high in life energy, with a good balance of macronutrients from which life energy will be efficiently extracted, and without needless excess calories. Notice I said "most of the time." This approach to eating is about viewing food primarily as fuel and energy to power your life—including your creative life—and choosing foods that provide high quality fuel. But that doesn't mean you need to deny yourself any "treat" food you really enjoy. It's fine to indulge in those kinds of foods occasionally—consistently denying yourself anything you find enjoyable is doomed to failure.

The key is to ensure that "most of the time" actually means "most of the time." When planning weekly meals and choosing daily foods, a good general guideline is to ensure that at least eighty percent or more of your meals and snacks over the course of week consist of fresh whole foods—complex carbohydrates with fiber, such as whole grains, fruits, and vegetables, lean protein, and a small amount of fat. Twenty percent or less of weekly meals and snacks should be foods considered indulgent or treats.

Moving. Breathing, drinking, eating—all of the activities we just discussed—channel necessary life force energy into the body. The body depends on these continual sources of energy to power the autonomic functions and physiological processes necessary for survival.

Notice there is a kind of hierarchy of need for these energy sources. For example, if you were to stop breathing, you would die in a matter of minutes. If you were to breathe but not drink water, you would die in a matter of days. If you were to breathe and drink water, but not take in nourishing food, life energy would flow for a longer period, but you would die within a matter of weeks.

To this basic hierarchy of need, we can add a fourth level: movement, or exercise. If you were to breathe, drink water, and eat nourishing food, you could survive for a long time, but if you did not move or exercise your body would eventually deteriorate to the point where it would simply lose function.

Our physical infrastructure—skeletal bones connected by joints, muscles, tendons, and ligaments interwoven with a network of arteries, veins, and capillaries that circulate blood, and neural pathways that send and receive messages from the brain—is constructed specifically to enable us to stand, walk, run, twist, bend, reach, lift, and throw. In other words, the body is designed to *move*, therefore it *must* move to remain healthy and ensure the efficient flow of energy.

In Part 2, we talked about the need for focused physical training to condition the body properly. Endurance athletes train specifically to acquire and maintain the energetic capacity to complete endurance events. As a *ChiWriter*, you do not need to physically train to that level or extent (unless you want to complete an endurance event), but a minimum of three hours (180 minutes) of moderate to intense physical activity, over the course of a week, is recommended to keep the body adequately conditioned, healthy, and energized.

Remember the training principle of consistency and frequency we talked about in Part 2: do not attempt to cram three hours of exercise into a weekend after remaining sedentary during the week. It is far better (and easier) to divide 180 minutes of weekly exercise into smaller increments throughout the week; for example, thirty-minute sessions six days a week, or perhaps three twenty-minute sessions during the week and two sixty-minute sessions over the weekend, depending on your schedule.

The day, time, duration, and type of workout each week should be planned so that you know when and how you will exercise. (You are far more likely to follow through if it's planned. We will talk about planning in the next section.) A key to success and longevity here is to choose activities that you enjoy: walking, running, biking, swimming, strength training, yoga, calisthenics, group exercise classes, or some combination of these activities.

Whatever activity you choose, the workout sessions should be moderate to vigorous in intensity, with brief periods of high intensity dialed in now and then to push your anaerobic threshold up. Of the total target workout time of 180 minutes a week, make ten percent of that time (or about eighteen minutes) high intensity intervals. For example, if you choose to walk briskly for thirty minutes six days a week, during three of those sessions, incorporate six, one-minute high intensity run intervals over the course of each thirty-minute workout: walk ten minutes to warm up, run one minute, walk two minutes to recover, and then repeat that cycle six times.

Of course, before starting any exercise program, you should talk to your doctor and get a complete physical exam, especially if you are deconditioned. If you are deconditioned, be sure to start slowly to avoid injury, adding length and intensity to your workouts gradually (over a matter of weeks) as your body adapts to the training.

At this point, you may be wondering how on earth you are going to find time to both exercise *and* write *and* fulfill all of your existing work and family obligations. You may be thinking if you could spend three hours exercising, wouldn't that time be better spent writing? My response is to remind you again that everything is connected, and that we are talking about energy management, not strictly time management.

Remember that you are not *spending* time exercising, you are *investing* time, and with any investment, a return is expected. The return you can expect on the time invested in exercising is far greater energy and productivity during the rest of your days and weeks — energy and productivity that will enable you to meet all of your obligations *and* move forward consistently on your writing goals.

Resting. The autonomic functions required for survival — respiration, circulation, digestion, neural activity, etc. — are hard work for the body and require continuous sources of energy derived from breathing, drinking, and eating. It's such hard work for the body, in fact, that we must spend around one-third of our lives sleeping to recover from it. Yet many people sacrifice sleep in the name of more time and greater productivity.

If we look at sleep from a traditional time-management perspective, we may think that shaving off an hour or two of sleep each night will give us more time and enable us to be more productive. Over the long term, though, this is counterproductive. Adequate sleep daily allows the body and mind to recover, recuperate, refresh, and reenergize, restoring physical and mental balance.

If you are physically deconditioned, eat a poor diet lacking in adequate nutrition or hydration, and remain sedentary most of the day, you are likely to feel fatigued and sluggish much of the time. You may feel the need and desire to sleep, but the sleep you take is probably not particularly restorative — it may be fitful, shallow, of poor quality. You may wake in the morning feeling as tired as you did when you went to bed. Because of poor sleep, you may continue to feel tired throughout the day, and lack resolve to exercise or eat properly, which only exacerbates and perpetuates this negative cycle.

What can you do?

Recognize that the quality of primary energy inputs throughout the day affects the quality of sleep and vice versa. When you breathe more deeply, stay well-hydrated, consume high-quality, nutrient-dense foods, and condition the body through exercise, you will have greater energy. When you have greater energy during awake hours, you will naturally enjoy deeper rest during sleep hours as the body seeks to recover and restore itself.

Deeper, more restful sleep (most of us need seven to eight hours of sleep every day) helps sustain greater energy during waking hours. Ensuring adequate physical rest, therefore, is essential to maximizing energy and optimizing daily energy management, which enables greater productivity. In turn, greater productivity supports your creative goals.

There is another form of rest that we humans are in a unique position to utilize and that is mental rest. Humans, of course, are differentiated from other living organisms (through which chi also flows) by a highly developed volitional consciousness, the ability to perceive, think, and make individual choices and decisions based on reason and cognitive inputs, rather than rely solely on instincts.

We not only have thoughts, we can *think* about those thoughts. We can be aware of the thoughts we're thinking and, with that awareness, we can shift from thoughts that do not serve us to thoughts that better serve us and move us forward rather than hold us back. In this way, changing our thoughts actually changes our lives. This unique metacognitive ability of humans makes another aspect and practice of optimizing energy management important: meditation and quiet reflection.

Meditation—the practice of sitting quietly, body relaxed and free of physical tension, and allowing your mental/emotional state to calm and still itself—is to the mind what exercise is to the body. As exercise conditions the body to perform more efficiently, so does meditation condition the mind to perform more efficiently. For many of us, our daily mental/emotional states are characterized by myriad racing thoughts about our many duties, obligations, challenges, responsibilities, and competing priorities, interlaced with assorted junk thoughts, fears, worries, anxieties, insecurities, and negative self-talk.

Earlier, we talked about the fact that when you eat junk food, your body uses the same physiological processes to extract energy from that junk as it would for healthy food—except that there's very little energy (nutritional content) to extract and your body suffers functionally as a result. Junk thoughts are like junk food—they utilize the same mental processes, the same neural pathways in the brain are activated, except that there's very little "nutritional content" in those thoughts and their energy is negative not positive. The effect is as predictable and inevitable as the effect of a steady diet of junk food on the body: your mind, your mental/emotional state, is not "fed" in the proper way and becomes ill-equipped to carry out its normal functions in the most efficient way.

Meditation reduces the amount of energy squandered by mentally racing through your day and dwelling on junk thoughts that don't support your goals. It helps condition the mind to think deliberately, positively, expansively, creatively. Many people who try meditation, however, claim that it doesn't work for them because it's too difficult to shut down the thought process. Even if they try to sit quietly and think about nothing, their minds still race.

But meditation is not about trying to think about nothing for a period of time. It's about using your metacognitive ability to observe your thoughts objectively rather than identify with them. Whatever thoughts come up, instead of latching onto them and letting them take your mind elsewhere—such as into a space of worry or fear or anxiety—take a step back and become aware of them without dwelling on them.

Simply observe your thoughts without judgment and without feeding them more mental energy. Over time, with practice, identifying as the observer of your thoughts, rather than as the thinker of those thoughts, opens up space between the thought itself and you as the thinker. Within that space you will find a greater sense of calm, peace, power, inspiration, even joy, because the "you" who is observing is observing from a higher realm of consciousness that the "you" who is thinking. In opening up that space, you are opening a channel for the energy of that higher consciousness to flow into your experience.

This is why time investment in meditation and quiet reflection can pay huge dividends in terms of the positive mental energy necessary to remain productive and moving toward your goals each day. Investing as little as five to ten minutes a day is all it takes to make a difference.

Simply choose a time when you won't be interrupted (for example, early morning before the demands of the day begin) and sit comfortably. Take a few deep, slow breaths in through the nose and out through the mouth as you mentally scan your body for any physical tension. As you exhale, release any physical tension so that your entire body is as relaxed as possible.

Then, become the *observer*, not the *thinker*. When your mind offers up a thought, acknowledge it, observe it without judgment, and allow it to drift away. This may be difficult at first, just as physical exertion is difficult when starting an exercise program from a deconditioned state; but with time and practice, it will become easier as your mind becomes better conditioned.

You can even practice this meditative technique for short periods three or four times a day by combining it with the other energetic practices we talked about previously. At regular intervals throughout your day, particularly if you have a sedentary job, take a short break for a physical and mental "reboot." Stretch and walk, feel the energy of movement in your limbs. Then, relax, close your eyes, and take several slow, deep breaths. As you breathe, slowly and deeply, quiet the mind by becoming the observer. After a minute or two, hydrate by mindfully drinking a cup of cool water. Be fully present as you swallow the water, feel it in your throat, and visualize its energy expanding in your body.

Review

We have now discussed the foundational practices essential to optimizing the physical and mental energy required to maintain the habits of mind and the habits of action necessary to achieve your writing goals. Before we move on, let's review what we've covered:

The reason most people fail to achieve a goal they've set is that they fail to effectively bridge the gap between the point of commitment and the point at which autotelic momentum, rather than pure discipline, begins to drive their efforts. They tend to either underestimate the difficulty involved in bridging that gap or overestimate their ability to do so. So they give up the struggle and return to old patterns of living that do not support their goal. Effectively bridging this gap can be supported by adopting the same three habits of mind that successful endurance athletes use:

1. The actions required to reach your goal are seen as integrated into your life, not as separate add-ons;

2. You are "in training" as a writer all the time, not just during the time you actually sit down to write. Every other activity in your life is connected to your goal and seen as supporting its achievement;

3. You manage energy, not just time. Since everything is connected at an energetic level, time invested in optimizing energy is critical. The return on that time investment is much greater energy that can be devoted to your goal. With much greater energy, you naturally become much more time-efficient and productive in all life domains.

Your body is constantly managing and regulating its utilization of energy based upon the inputs it receives from you. Whether you realize it or not, every time you breathe, eat, drink, move, or sleep you are making choices that dramatically affect your physical and mental energy (and thus your creative energy since everything is connected); it therefore makes sense to make these choices consciously, with the intent to optimize your energy. Five key practices, integrated into your daily life, will achieve this:

1. Breathing: several times a day, practice breathing slowly, deeply, consciously.

2. Hydrating: a few times a day, mindfully drink a cup of pure water.

3. Fueling: eat mostly whole foods that grow, not foods that are manufactured or overly processed. Foods that are grown have life energy in them that manufactured, overly processed foods do not.

4. Moving: Regularly engage in exercise that strengthens and conditions the body to perform more effectively. Aim for

180 minutes per week, spread out over five to six days of moderate to vigorous activity.

5. Resting: See adequate rest as vital to your physical and mental conditioning. Aim for seven to eight hours of sleep daily. Engage in mental rest, too, by sitting quietly, relaxed, for five to ten minutes daily and become the observer, not the thinker.

If all five of these energetic components are in balance and of high quality—in other words if chi is operating at optimally efficient levels in your life—then you will enjoy higher levels of energy, vitality, and overall well-being and the natural result will be greater focus and productivity in all of your life domains.

Notice how the three habits of mind and these five key energetic practices are synergistic and mutually supportive: If you view your writing goal through the paradigm of these three habits of mind, you will more naturally view these five practices as necessary to and supportive of your creative work. And if you view these five practices as necessary to and supportive of your creative work, you will more easily sustain the habits of mind that support your writing goals.

Applying the *ChiWriting* Principles

Essentially, these three habits of mind and the five practices for optimizing life energy provide a strong foundation, the energetic bedrock upon which to build the integrated structure necessary to apply the *ChiWriting* principles, without sacrificing important goals and responsibilities in other life domains. Let's quickly review the *ChiWriting* principles we discussed in Part 2.

The five key *planning principles* are:

1. Define the major seasonal goal. Athletes in most any sport train by season (usually annually) and the major goal for the season is defined. The athlete has a definite primary event in mind as the major goal for the season, which means there is a specific future date (the event date) by which the athlete needs to be fully conditioned and ready to compete.

2. Define interim seasonal goals. Athletes frequently schedule interim events as a way of testing the efficacy of the training plan. For example, an athlete whose seasonal goal is to complete the Boston Marathon might incorporate competition in shorter events — a 10K, a half-marathon — into her training plan to fine tune race strategy, conditioning, and performance.

3. Utilize "periodization." Periodization structures training over specific periods or phases to ensure that conditioning progresses appropriately and peaks at the most appropriate times.

4. Develop a specific, written training plan. The effective athlete will create a specific written seasonal/monthly/weekly/daily training plan utilizing specific workouts on a consistent basis in order to be sure she is ready to compete come race day. This plan is also important in tracking progress to ensure any necessary adjustments are made along the way.

5. Have a goal for every workout. Once an overall plan is in place, athletes structure each individual workout to accomplish a specific goal that supports achievement of the overall desired outcome.

The five key *training principles* are:

1. Train consistently and frequently. The endurance athlete knows that training the body and its energy systems consistently and frequently is a better path to success than focusing solely on the total volume (amount) of training. The endurance athlete knows she cannot simply train on weekends or wait until a few weeks out and then start training and expect to be successful on race day.

2. Incorporate rest and recovery. The endurance athlete knows that recovery—periods of rest, sleep, and less intensive physical effort—are as important as periods of active physical training. He knows the body's adaptations to training only happen during recovery periods, when the body rebuilds.

3. Utilize coaching and/or team support. The endurance athlete understands the high value of coaching and/or team-based training. He knows that working with others and being accountable to others for his efforts keeps his commitment level high. He knows that leveraging the support and expertise of others will further his goals more efficiently and powerfully.

4. Train mentally as well as physically. The endurance athlete utilizes mental training as well as physical training. She knows that mental conditioning is just as important as physical conditioning for success.

5. Recognize the importance of diet and nutrition. The endurance athlete knows the critical role nutrition plays in fueling the body properly for maintaining and enhancing the energy levels required of both training workouts and race competition.

Applying these principles to writing and developing your creative mind will lead you systematically toward the completion of your goal to write a book. You are going to use them to create a structure and action habits that will move you forward. When you reviewed these principles, did you notice how many are naturally supported by the three habits of mind and the five practices for optimizing your life energy discussed in the prior section?

For example, you are going to automatically practice most of the training principles simply by fueling and hydrating your body properly, getting adequate rest, meditating, and so on, which will not only optimize your available energy but also further integrate into your busy life the planning, structure, and action habits necessary to make consistent progress on your book.

In Part 2, I recommended a minimum time investment of fifteen hours weekly devoted to the mental and physical activities necessary to write your book: six hours of writing workouts, six hours of reading, and three hours of moderate to intense physical exercise. It would be difficult to consistently invest that amount of time weekly through traditional time-management techniques alone. But you can do it through energy management and effective planning. Planning is key.

Planning Creates Structure, Structure Creates Progress

Once you utilize the three key habits of mind and the five key energetic practices to create a solid energetic foundation to build upon, you will develop a structure to focus that energy specifically toward your goal. By "structure" here I mean a spatial and temporal structure—anchor points in space and time for accomplishing certain important tasks and actions, i.e., knowing what to do, and when and where to do it. A written plan is key for creating that structure.

A written plan is a roadmap, a visual depiction of the way forward; it describes the line of sight between where you are now and where you want to be and how you will get there. It also makes it much easier to track progress and make necessary adjustments along the way to ensure you remain on track. Therefore, the fourth planning principle—develop a specific, written training plan—is vitally important to successfully implementing each of the other planning and training principles.

In the Appendix are sample season and weekly training plan templates for your book. These planning templates use an "at-a-glance" format incorporating all of the four remaining necessary elements for a plan/structure for moving consistently toward your goal, including a definite end date (the date by which you will have completed your book), periodization (or phases of training that accomplish specific or targeted objectives), interim goals (checkpoints along the way to your ultimate destination), weekly training volumes, and defined daily workouts (what you are actually going to do each day to move forward in your creative conditioning/book development). This includes not just your writing workouts, but also your physical workouts, and your reading time investment. As we've discussed, these are also essential to supporting your writing goal.

You may find these templates helpful, or you may choose another method. A written training plan can be developed and maintained in a variety of ways that suit your personal preferences. If you already use and are comfortable with some type of calendaring or planning system—whether digital or paper-based—to keep track of important goals, activities, appointments, and dates in other life domains, you may prefer to incorporate training for your book into your existing system. Or you may prefer to maintain a planning system for your book training that is separate from your existing system—that's fine too, as long as you integrate it into your planning activities in other life domains.

Whatever type of calendering system or planning format you choose, the important thing is to define and write down each element of your plan, beginning with your desired outcome.

Part 3: Becoming a ChiWriter

Season Planning

Structure and planning are vitally important to the *ChiWriter*, just as it is for the endurance athlete. Every good plan, as Stephen Covey said, begins with the end in mind. Choose a date when your "season" will end, i.e., the date of your "big event," the achievement of your goal, the completion of your book. Starting backward from this planned date of accomplishment, map out blocks of time structured to systematically move you toward that goal.

As we've discussed, endurance athletes, whether amateur or professional, typically plan and train according to a "season," which generally plays out over the course of a year and includes progressive phases of conditioning, a schedule of actual races and events in which to compete leading up to the main event, as well as off-season weeks or months. They know when their key races are and they build their training program around them.

For example, an amateur marathoner whose goal is to qualify and compete in the Boston Marathon, held in late April, might build her season around completing that goal, so her training plan would be focused on making her mentally and physically ready come the race date. But since runners must qualify for the Boston Marathon, her training plan would also need to factor in training to ensure readiness for the event that will qualify her for Boston — perhaps a sanctioned event in the fall.

Working backward then from her main goal in late April, she might build a training program that encompasses a "season" of perhaps nine to ten months, which would include several months of focused, progressive training leading up to the qualifying event in the fall, and another several months of training leading up to the Boston Marathon.

To use an example from another endurance sport, a professional triathlete might begin a ten-month long season in January, training and competing at different events to hone and test his skills and conditioning, leading up to and culminating in the ultimate goal of competing in the Ironman World Championships, held in Kona, Hawaii in October. The "off-season" in both examples would encompass two or three months during which specific event training is scaled back to allow the body and mind to fully recover and reenergize before a new season begins.

This "season planning" paradigm can be applied to your writing life, only your goal, of course, is to finish and submit a book. So the first step in the *ChiWriting* planning process is to pick your season—starting with the date you want to finish your book. Let's say you want to write a novel and there is a novel writing contest with a submission deadline of November 1. You might pick October 31 as the definite date you will have your novel finished and submitted to the contest. Now that you have established the outcome (i.e., beginning with the end in mind), you can plan and schedule backward from there—just as endurance athletes do when planning for their seasonal main events.

The final day of your writing season does not have to coincide with an external deadline necessarily, but having an external deadline in mind can provide additional motivation that helps keep your plan on track. If there is no appropriate external deadline available, choose any reasonable date in the future, on which date you plan to have your book finished and ready for submissions. Treat this as a firm deadline and work consistently and frequently to meet it.

If you were running a marathon to be held on October 15th you would know absolutely, positively that you would need to be ready that day. That same certainty should be applied to the deadline for finishing your book—no matter what date you choose or whether it is internally or externally driven, you know that that is the "deadline" for your book, the date it will be complete and ready to be sent out into the world. How long your season is, i.e., how far in advance you pick a finish date, depends on a number of factors, but I would suggest a minimum of nine to ten months if you are starting from scratch.

Let's say you decide your writing season will begin on January 1 and end October 31 when you know you will submit a manuscript to a contest, a publisher, or agent. You now know your writing season will be ten months, or forty-four weeks, long:

January					February				March					April				May				
1	2	3	4	5	6	7	8	9	10	11	12	13	14	15	16	17	18	19	20	21	22	23
June				July				August					September				October					
24	25	26	27	28	29	30	31	32	33	34	35	36	37	38	39	40	41	42	43	44		

You will divide this forty-four week season into distinct periods or phases, each of which will have a specific purpose in moving you progressively toward your ultimate goal. Before we cover this "periodization" concept and how it applies to the *ChiWriter*, I want to emphasize the scalability of the seasonal approach to planning.

Your "season" can be scaled up or down, depending on the scope and complexity of your projects. For many projects, a single forty-four week season may be enough to achieve your goal. For others, it may be too long or not long enough. If you are writing a short novella, for example, a single season of, say, twenty-four weeks might be adequate.

Or, if you are planning a long historical novel, you may estimate that your book is going to take four years to complete. In that case, you can view each annual "season" as a single period or phase of training. This is what Olympic endurance athletes do. They have single season training plans, but each season is a component of an overall four-year plan to compete in the Olympic Games. You may also be wondering what happens if you "miss" your season deadline or your writing season doesn't turn out to be long enough to finish your book. The answer is simple: You keep going.

If you originally planned to complete your book within a single ten-month season, but instead only completed half of your book by season's end, that is *not* a reason to give up in frustration. You may have reached only fifty percent of your goal, but that's probably 100 percent more than you would have had if you had not planned and trained all season. Simply reassess and plan your next season based on what you've already accomplished.

Periodization, or Phase Planning
Having defined the length of your season, you divide that period into phases. You can build these phases in whatever way or number makes sense for your particular project. At a minimum, I would recommend four phases that are essentially analogous to how an endurance athlete "periodizes," or structures training phases.

The athlete would focus the first phase on developing a base level of conditioning; the second phase would build on that base to develop event-specific strengths; the third phase would focus on "peak" conditioning, with training designed to hone endurance to event-level readiness; and, finally, a taper phase during which training volume is dialed back somewhat prior to the event so that training adaptations are fully assimilated into the body and the athlete is fresh and rested heading into the big event.

As a *ChiWriter*, you will follow a similar progression. Using our example of a forty-four-week long writing season from January 1 to October 31, you might structure a four-phase training plan by dividing the season into periods of time during which you will achieve similar objectives in terms of progressive creative conditioning and completing a manuscript; for example: a sixteen-week base phase; twelve weeks each for the build and peak phases; and a four-week taper phase, as shown:

January					February				March					April				May				
1	2	3	4	5	6	7	8	9	10	11	12	13	14	15	16	17	18	19	20	21	22	23
Phase 1: Base																	Phase 2: Build				

June				July				August					September				October			
24	25	26	27	28	29	30	31	32	33	34	35	36	37	38	39	40	41	42	43	44
Build (cont.)				Phase 3: Peak													Phase 4: Taper			

Phase 1: Base (Sixteen Weeks). The base training phase is about building your foundation; laying the groundwork for subsequent phases. During this phase, training will be focused on putting together as much material as possible. You want to get as much material down on paper or digitally as possible, not worrying at this point about mistakes, grammar, spelling, or structure.

The goal of this phase is just to get it down, to have the raw material to work with — remember "writing is revising," and you cannot work the material and revise it in later phases if it is not first captured on paper (or digitally). This phase also conditions you to avoid writer's block. In terms of creative conditioning, this is the phase in which you are training your internal editor to quiet down, to back off for a while, and get yourself adapted to the ritual and routine of your writing practice (i.e., your daily "workouts").

If your book requires a lot of research — for example, you're writing a historical novel and need to know more about the historical setting of your book, or you're writing a nonfiction book and need to learn more about your topic — your initial phase might be focused on achieving the research outcomes necessary to move on to the next phase.

Some writers like to work from an outline. Others prefer to jump in and see where the writing takes them before they begin to structure and shape the material. There is no right or wrong answer; both ways are fine. But if outlining is your preferred method, you might also consider a shorter "pre-conditioning" phase (say, a week or two) during which you map out the structure of your book in advance before you move into base training.

Phase 2: Build (Twelve Weeks). During the build phase, you continue to build on your material; you go back and refine what you have and add new material based on how the book is shaping up. The goal of the build phase is to continue your creative conditioning by focusing on the "big picture" of your book—structure, story arc, character development, voice, flow, and so on—not so much on details like grammar or spelling.

During this phase, your internal editor is still in the background; you are still not worrying too much about small mistakes or how "good" or how "rough" your draft is; it's supposed to be rough. By the time you reach the peak phase you've substantially framed out the book, and it's time to further shape and define the material.

Phase 3: Peak (Twelve Weeks). During the peak phase, your book takes its final shape. The structure is becoming defined and solidified and you are mastering character, voice, flow, and content; you are in control of the material. Here is where your internal editor comes back into play, only now it's not there to harangue you, it's there to help you correct, refine, revise, edit, restructure, as needed. You expand content where you need to and delete content if you have to. The book begins to near completion.

Phase 4 Taper (Four Weeks). For the endurance athlete, the taper phase is focused on ensuring optimal event-day readiness. She steps back somewhat from the rigors of training to allow the body to completely assimilate the training. By dialing back the volume of workouts somewhat while maintaining some training intensity, the athlete accomplishes the dual goals of allowing the body more time to fully adapt to the training while honing and sharpening event-readiness. By the day of the event, the body is fresh, rested, and conditioning level is finely tuned and ready to go.

Similarly, as a *ChiWriter*, you will use this taper phase to focus on final refinements to your manuscript. This is the phase where you will step back somewhat from normal training routines while maintaining intensity focused on becoming "event-ready." Dialing back the training volume allows you to return to the manuscript with fresh eyes, while honing and sharpening the book through proofreading, corrections, line edits, or other final changes. By the time your "event" arrives — the deadline you based your plan on — your book is complete and ready to go out into the world.

Once season and phase planning is complete — once you know your broad goals and what you need to accomplish during each phase to progress — it is time to plan weekly.

Weekly Planning

Once you know how you will "periodize" your season — or the time you have until your planned deadline arrives — you will begin weekly planning sessions. Once a week at a convenient time (perhaps on Sunday evening before your work week begins), you will put a plan together for how you will move forward that week.

Look at your week ahead and decide how and when you are going to complete a minimum of six hours of writing volume, six hours of reading, and three hours of exercise. Which of the three basic writing workouts will you use and what days and times will they occur? When will you read and exercise?

Ideally, you will develop a set time and space for your writing workouts, reading, and exercise that establishes a consistent routine for each. At the outset of your season and periodized plan, however, it is impossible to tell what each week will bring in terms of obligations, events, and obstacles that come up that could potentially derail your overall plan. So it's important to revisit your plan each week and come up with a sub-plan that takes into account all of your known commitments and responsibilities for the upcoming week.

What meetings and appointments do you have scheduled? What work projects do you need to complete? Where and when do you need to shuttle your kids that week? When will you spend time with your significant other? As you answer these questions and block out time on your calendar accordingly, keep in mind the three habits of mind: Integrate, don't add; stay "in training;" and manage energy, not just time.

Look at your entire week holistically and plan your daily writing workouts accordingly. If possible, plan the weekly schedule of all your major goals, tasks, and activities around your planned writing workouts.

If that is not possible, and sometimes it won't be, then still schedule your writing workouts in somewhere. Do not let the need to change your daily writing schedule be a reason to abandon your writing schedule altogether. Neither do you want to skip your writing workouts during the week and try to cram on the weekend. Remember that consistent and frequent workouts are key to the creative conditioning process—just as they are to physical conditioning—and critically important in building the overall volume necessary to progress effectively.

This weekly planning session need not take long. Ten or fifteen minutes invested on a Sunday evening, for example, will help ensure you stay on track with your writing plan. And, it will also pay the extra dividend of enhanced productivity in your work and family domains.

During these weekly planning sessions, map out how you intend to reach your overall writing volume goal for that week, as well as your reading and exercise volumes (again, a minimum of six, six, and three hours, respectively). As you do this and schedule in your daily workouts for the week, you will practice another one of the five key planning principles: Have a goal for every workout. On any given day, will you complete a high-intensity writing workout, a tempo workout, or a long, slow distance workout?

During a busy work week, for example, you might schedule shorter high-intensity or tempo writing sessions totaling two or three hours, and longer sessions on the weekend totaling three or four hours to meet the minimum goal of six hours of creative conditioning time. On some days, you might schedule two-a-day workouts—say, a fifteen- minute high intensity writing session first in the morning and a thirty- or forty-five-minute tempo session in the evening before bed.

You might also schedule a "brick" workout—one type of workout immediately followed by a different type of workout. Occasionally on a weekend day (or a day when you have few other obligations), you might schedule in a "Big Day," a six- to eight-hour long, slow distance session. Two-a-day, brick, and Big Day workouts are strategies that many endurance athletes employ in their training plans that can also work for you as a *ChiWriter*. (We will talk further about these workout strategies in the next section.)

Don't neglect to schedule in a recovery day. The endurance athlete regularly takes a day off—usually once a week— to allow his body to recover and adapt. The *ChiWriter* should do the same. For the athlete, a lack of adequate recovery time can result in over-training; a counterproductive state in which conditioning, growth, and progress all suffer. In an overtrained state, performance and overall capacity, rather than improving, degrades over time.

Although writing obviously is not as physically demanding as endurance training, it is nonetheless creatively, mentally, even emotionally demanding; your creative mind also needs rest and recovery to adapt to the demands placed upon it. Allowing time for the creative mind to rest, recover, and adapt, to prepare itself for further greater effort, is a valuable and necessary part of training

ChiWriting

as a *ChiWriter*, and it will enable you to return to your material refreshed, which will enhance productivity.

In her excellent book *The Artist's Way*, Julia Cameron writes of a similar concept she calls "Artist Dates," one day per week during which she recommends artists devote time to imaginative play or fun activities not directly connected to their normal creative work in order to replenish the "inner well of images and inspiration."

Below is an example of what a typical weekly schedule might look like. It incorporates each type of workout and meets the recommended writing, reading, and exercise volumes.

Monday	Tuesday	Wednesday	Thursday	Friday	Saturday	Sunday	Weekly Volume
Write :15 HIW :30 TW	Write :15 HIW	Write :45 TW	Write :15 HIW :30 TW	Write OFF	Write 2:00 LSDW	Write 1:30 LSDW	Write 6:00
Read :30	Read :60	Read :30	Read :30	Read 1:00	Read 1:00	Read 1:30	Read 6:00
Move :20	Move :20	Move :20	Move :20	Move OFF	Move :40	Move 1:00	Move 3:00
1:35	1:35	1:35	1:35	1:00	3:40	4:00	15:00

HIW = High Intensity Writing; TW = Tempo Writing; LSDW = Long, Slow Distance Writing

This example is illustrative, not prescriptive; obviously, you need to apply the *ChiWriting* principles in ways that suit your individual preferences and particular project and life circumstances at any given time. That's why weekly and daily planning in terms of how you'll consistently implement your overall plan is so important. Note that the writing workout types and daily volumes are flexible and can be adjusted in myriad ways that allow you to meet weekly volume goals while still enabling you to focus on commitments and responsibilities in other life domains.

We've talked about the importance of emphasizing energy management over time management in implementing your plan, but you'll still need to find the time, won't you? You'll need to find an hour or two on workdays, and three or fours hours each on weekend days (or the days you're off work) to devote to yourself and your writing, reading, and exercise goals as a *ChiWriter*.

How? How can you find (and then invest) this time and make it a priority? Most people lead busy lives. Between job, family, household, and other obligations, most would say it is difficult or impossible to find an extra two hours in their workdays. But of course, it's not. It's simply a matter of managing your energy, managing your choices, and allocating your time investments most effectively to ensure the greatest return. Here's how:

Bookend your days with time to yourself

The easiest, most effective way I've found of investing the time necessary to commit to your goal of writing a book is to employ a "bookending" strategy: begin and end your days with time to yourself. Give yourself at least two hours a day during the workweek: the first hour upon waking and the last hour before sleep. On the weekends (or the days you don't work), you can extend the time upon waking and before bedtime to two or three hours or more, depending on your schedule and workout goals.

The bulk of your days will still be devoted to fulfilling responsibilities in other life domains, but by bookending your days like this, you easily allot yourself the time you need as a *ChiWriter* (a minimum of fifteen hours weekly) to devote to writing, reading, and exercising.

As simple as this strategy is, however, it will likely require a change in your schedule. Here's where traditional time management can be used to effect this change: Let's say you normally get eight hours of sleep (most people need at least seven to eight hours) by going to bed at 11:00 p.m. and waking up at 7:00 a.m. to get ready for work.

With this bookending strategy, you would maintain a nightly eight hours of sleep (because adequate rest is vitally important) but you would shift your sleep schedule. Instead of 11:00 p.m. to

7:00 a.m., your normal sleep schedule would become 10:00 p.m. to 6:00 a.m. That gives you one extra hour in the morning before you need to get ready for the day—time you will now devote to yourself and your *ChiWriting* goals. You would also give yourself the hour immediately before bedtime—9:00 p.m. to 10:00 p.m.—for the same purpose.

On the weekends (or the days you don't work), it's best to maintain the same sleep schedule, but without normal work responsibilities, you can likely extend the time devoted to your writing goals. For example, on Saturday and Sunday mornings, your *ChiWriting* time investment might be extended to three or four hours, from 6:00 a.m. to 9:00 or 10:00 a.m. This gives you a solid chunk of productive time and still allows you to devote most of the weekend to your normal pursuits—family activities, household duties, recreation, etc.

I realize that shifting your sleep schedule and investing time immediately before and after sleep is easier said than done. It may take some getting used to. Your body may need to adjust and you may need to reduce or eliminate some evening activities that aren't as important as your goal of writing a book.

If you examine what you do in the early- to mid-evening hours, say between six p.m. and eleven p.m., there will be important activities like eating a good dinner, catching up with your spouse or partner, interacting with your kids, and relaxing after a demanding workday—all essential time investments. But there will also likely be some activities you could cut back on, like watching too much television, surfing the Internet, or scrolling through Facebook. Not to say you can't do these things at all, or that they aren't sometimes valuable as a means of necessary relaxation or maintaining social connections; but in terms of managing your evening time most effectively, you will need to reallocate that time to support your *ChiWriting* goals.

Consider 6:00 p.m. to 9:00 p.m., for example, the chunk of time you are allocating to important activities like the evening meal, relaxing, and investing time with your family. 9:00 p.m. to 10:00 p.m. then becomes the chunk of time before sleep that you devote to your book. Eight hours later, you will arise and devote another hour (at least) to your book before attending to other daily responsibilities.

Bookending is a simple concept, but effective when put into practice. Henceforth, these daily hours are *your* time, no one else's. In the hours just after waking and just before bed, you will focus solely on yourself and your *ChiWriting* goals: writing, reading, and exercising.

Now let's look at how the time invested with this daily bookending strategy might be structured.

Structuring your "bookends"

As a *ChiWriter*, you will practice the three habits of mind and the five energetic practices consistently throughout your days, but with the bookending strategy, you will invest time in the three specific *ChiWriting* activities: writing workouts (to condition the creative mind and put words on the page), reading (to properly fuel the creative mind), and physical exercise (to develop and maintain the necessary physical and mental energy to achieve your goals). The bookending strategy gives you two opportunities each day, a minimum of two hours each workday, and ideally longer on non-workdays, to invest in these three key activities.

How should this time be allocated? In the way that makes the most sense for you and your particular situation and preferences. Some writers prefer to write in the morning hours and others prefer evening hours. The bookending strategy is flexible enough to accommodate both types. For example, if you are a "morning" person (that is, you feel most creative and productive in the morning), you will likely benefit most from investing the first hour of your day in completing your writing and physical workouts and use the last hour of your day before sleep for reading. If, however, you feel more creative and productive as a writer during the evening hours, you will likely benefit most from completing your daily writing workouts in the hour before bedtime, and perhaps reading as well, while using your morning hour for exercise.

During your weekly planning session, you will look at the week ahead and decide how each of your daily "bookends" will be structured and what you will accomplish during these time investments.

I, myself, am a morning person, so I tend to schedule most of my writing and physical workouts during the first hour of the day, and reading during the last hour (although I am flexible depending on what is going in other areas of my life on any given day). Below is an example of how the first and last hours of a typical weekday might be structured to include both a high-intensity writing session and exercise, based on what I, as a morning person, have done in the past. (I tend to schedule tempo writing workouts of thirty to forty-five minutes on days that I don't physically exercise, or on days that are more flexible schedule-wise, and typically schedule long slow distance writing workouts on the weekends when I can invest more time).

The First Hour

:00-:05 Wake, rise, stretch, breathe deeply; walk to the kitchen, drink a cup of water, pour some coffee (I have my coffeemaker preset to have coffee ready when I wake up), breathe deeply some more, be mindful, sip your coffee, practice gratefulness, become the observer.

:05-:10 Head to your writing space—a room or space you have set aside for your writing workouts—sit down, get

Part 3: Becoming a ChiWriter

yourself comfortable, don't rush, be mindful of your movements. These physical, mechanical movements you make every day to head to your writing space will become part of your pre-writing ritual and will serve to prepare your creative mind for your writing workout, much like an endurance athlete "warms up" before a physical workout (more on this later). Open your notebook or computer file.

:10-:15 Once you're comfortable, pen and notebook or computer file at the ready, spend a few minutes reading over what you've written before—that will also serve to prime the creative pump. If you want to make a few notes or corrections or additions as you read, that's fine, but don't spend too much time doing this, the objective of reading your prior day's work is to move your creative mind definitively into the writing process, to warm up your creative muscles just as an athlete warms up muscles before a workout. Once you are at your starting place again, begin a high-intensity writing session.

:15-:30 Start writing using your pen or keyboard, write quickly, without stopping to edit or correct, keep moving; don't listen to your internal editor at this point, just keep getting the words down in whatever order, shape, or flow they come. At the end of fifteen minutes, close your notebook or file. Depending on how fast you write or type, you could now have up to a few hundred words of raw material to work with. But at this point, do not go read back over your work.

:30-:35 You have finished your writing workout for the day. Take a moment to reflect positively on this outcome. Rise and stretch and feel the satisfaction of having committed raw material to the page. Smile to yourself.

Pat yourself on the back. Give yourself that mental reward. Stretch and breathe deeply and feel your breath filling your body. Then prepare to finish out the hour by transitioning to exercise.

:35-:55 Use the next fifteen- to twenty-minute chunk of time to move, to get your heart rate up. You could walk or jog, jump on an elliptical machine or treadmill if you have one, do calisthenics. The objective is to increase your body's energy level for the day—and to condition your body over time.

:55-1:00 Use the final few minutes to meditate; relax and get mindful again, close your eyes, feel your heart rate coming back down following your exercise, at the same time, feel the energy you've created flowing through your body. Breathe deeply, slowly. Be grateful. Then move on with your day.

The Second Hour

:00-:05 Stop what you're doing (shut off the TV, put your smartphone down, etc.) and prepare for your nightly routine; be mindful, breathe deeply for a couple minutes, practice gratefulness, become the observer.

:05-:10 Head to your reading space—a favorite chair, your bedroom—sit down, get yourself comfortable, don't rush, be mindful of your movements. Open your book or e-reader.

:10-:45 Invest thirty- to thirty-five minutes (more, if possible) reading—poetry, fiction, nonfiction, memoir, biography, etc. I like to keep a pen and a journal or notepad handy because reading another writer's work will often provoke ideas and insights into my own work, so I jot them down.

:45-:55   Perform your regular sleep hygiene habits — wash your face, brush your teeth, slip into your sleep attire, climb into bed, and be mindful through all these actions.

:55-1:00   Use the last few minutes of the day to breathe deeply and reflect on the day, letting go of the day's frustrations or irritations and practicing gratefulness, then easing into a meditative state that allows sleep to take over.

Of course, these are illustrative examples; they're not meant to be strictly prescriptive, you can structure your bookends however you like as long as you are progressing toward your goals. You might, for example, exercise first thing in the morning and then move into your writing space to complete your writing workout, depending on your preference. Or you might practice your sleep hygiene habits before you invest time reading.

Also, you do not need to plan your hours out minute-by-minute, as I have it laid out above; the objective is simply to develop productive routines during each bookend that move you through these hours with intention, in a way that moves you progressively toward your goals. Regardless of how your morning time is structured, for example, you can move forward with the rest of your day with the satisfaction of knowing that you've accomplished at least two important *ChiWriting* goals: conditioning your creative mind by creating words on the page to work with, and conditioning your body through movement and exercise. Similarly, regardless of how your evening time is structured, you can ease into sleep with the satisfaction and peace of mind of knowing that you've completed reading that is helping to fuel your creative mind and support your writing.

You may be reading this and thinking, "I'm just not a morning person." I wasn't always a morning person, either. For years, it was difficult for me to wake up in the morning. Like many people, I'd hit the snooze button once too often, so that when I did finally get up I was already in a rush—get showered, dressed, gulp down some coffee, herd the kids to school, fight traffic, etcetera. By the time I arrived at work, booted up my computer, got more coffee, and chatted with coworkers before finally starting work on a project or task, I'd been up at least two hours and nothing much had been accomplished.

If this sounds familiar to you, imagine how much better it would be if, instead of a morning of stress-filled frenzy, you started the day quietly, intentionally, with a mindful routine that enables you to accomplish some of your most important mission-oriented goals before giving up the rest of the day in service to the expectations of others. This is what implementing the bookending strategy did for me.

Although getting up an hour earlier every day took some getting used to in the beginning, it worked out well for me and made a huge difference. In fact, it worked so well that I eventually expanded my morning time to two hours. My normal routine now is to arise in the morning at least two hours before I have to start getting ready for any work or family obligations for that day (for me, that's usually around 5:00 a.m.), I now look forward to it—it has become an autotelic experience for me.

Within my two hours, I typically invest chunks of time in reading, in writing, in exercising, and in meditating; that's a lot, but the two hours bookend I give myself also feels leisurely; I don't feel rushed in getting those things done that I want to accomplish; instead, I move slowly, mindfully, enjoying the peace and quiet of the dark early morning, puttering, easing into each of the things I want to do.

It's a wonderful way to start the day and I really can't imagine going back to the days when I slept in as long as possible before jumping out of bed and rushing through the morning to get to work. It feels to me like an incredible luxury to have that time alone in the mornings to focus on myself and my goals. Likewise with the hour before bedtime. Give yourself that gift with the first and last hours of your day.

Review

In the previous section, we covered the three habits of mind and the five energetic practices that are foundational to the *ChiWriting* process. They will enable you to optimize your available energy and integrate into your busy life the planning, structure, and action habits necessary to make consistent progress on your book. Developing a written plan is key because it creates structure, and structure creates progress:

- **Plan your season:** Begin with the end in mind. When will your season end? Pick a date that works for you or an external date, such as a contest deadline, that can help keep you on track. I recommend a "season" of about nine to ten months, which can be scaled down to a number of weeks or up across multiple seasons, depending on the project.

- **Periodize your plan:** Divide your season into phases, periods of time focused on a specific goal or purpose that will move you progressively toward your season objective. If your book takes longer than one season, simply divide multiple seasons into periodized, progressive phases.

- **Plan weekly:** Once you define your season and its periodized phases, sit down weekly to plan each day of the coming week and which workouts you will accomplish on each day. Be flexible and take into account family and work responsibilities or other obligations.

- **"Bookend" your days:** During the workweek, devote the first and last hours of your day to *ChiWriting* activities—writing workouts, physical workouts, and reading. On weekends (or non-workdays), expand these bookends to two or three hours or more, as your schedule allows.

Following this planning strategy will enable you to invest at least fifteen hours per week to your writing goals—including writing workouts, reading, and physical exercise—and still allow you to meet other important family and work responsibilities. Depending on how you plan your phases, weeks, and daily schedule, you could accomplish two or three high intensity writing workouts (fifteen to twenty minutes each), two or three tempo writing workouts (thirty to forty-five minutes each), and one or two long slow distance writing workouts (two- to three-plus hours each), potentially yielding ten to fifteen pages of writing per week within a total of about six hours of writing time.

More Training Tips:
Additional Strategies to Support Your Goals

We have talked about three habits of mind and five energetic practices as being essential for *ChiWriters*. These habits of mind (integrate don't add; stay in training; and manage energy, not just time) and the five energetic practices (deep breathing, proper hydration, eating mostly whole foods, moving and exercising, and getting adequate sleep and rest, including mental rest through meditation) provide a strong foundation for maintaining and enhancing energy levels and supporting the planning, structure, and action habits necessary to achieve your writing goals.

Part 3: Becoming a ChiWriter

To further strengthen the foundation and move you further along the path toward your writing goals, there are several other supplementary tips and strategies you can use, as you see fit, to help integrate *ChiWriting* principles into your life. These tips and strategies are also drawn from the world of endurance training and can be employed in analogous ways. They include:

- Warming up
- Skill drills
- Two-a-day workouts
- The "Brick" workout
- The "Big Day"

Let's look at each one in more detail.

Warming Up

Before a workout, the endurance athlete "warms up." She goes through a series of movements at a slow pace for a short period of time to increase blood flow to muscles and joints. Physically, this prepares the body for the more intense work to come and helps protects against injury. It also serves to prepare the athlete mentally, putting her into a state of mind that supports the physical effort and enhancing the potential for entering into a flow state during the actual workout.

The *ChiWriter* can also "warm up" and derive the same benefits from this process: preparing the creative mind for the more intense work to come and enhancing the potential for entering into a flow state during the writing workout. For the *ChiWriter*, the key to warming up is to develop a consistent pre-writing routine or ritual that will serve as a signal to the creative mind that it is about to get down to business. This pre-writing routine need not be anything elaborate; it can be quite simple.

During a talk I once heard from author Sena Jeter Naslund, she described her own pre-writing ritual as a "mechanical process," consisting simply of being conscious of the movements it took her to rise from her bed in the morning and make her way to her writing desk: She swiveled up from her bed, put her feet on the floor, rose, walked to her kitchen, took a coffee mug from the cupboard, poured hot coffee, took the steaming cup to her study, set the cup down on her desk, and sat down. All of these simple, mechanical movements were done deliberately, consciously, with the mindful intention of preparing herself to write, of signaling her creative mind that it would soon be called upon to perform.

Dr. Naslund's talk was something of a revelation to me, and as a result, my own morning experience was transformed. I did not change much about the way I wake up and start my time alone in the mornings—I rise, walk to the kitchen, let the dogs outside, drink a cup of water, pour some coffee, walk outside for a few minutes to breathe deeply; I then walk back inside, feed the dogs, and make my way to my home office—but what changed was my consciousness of this "mechanical process." I began to impart the mindful intention that these simple, functional movements were "warming up" my creative mind, preparing it for the workout to come.

You can do the same. Whether you perform your writing workouts primarily during the first bookended hour of your day or the last, begin to create for yourself a pre-writing "warm up" routine with the conscious intention of signaling your creative mind to prepare for the writing workout that is about to begin. In this way, the mechanical process of preparing to write becomes part of the creative process, making it much easier to maintain consistent action, ease into the writing workout, and help transform it into an autotelic experience.

Skill Drills

Endurance athletes use drills—a series of specific movements designed to improve particular skills or body mechanics—as part of their training regimen to enhance overall performance. An athlete's typical workout might include: a warm up, the actual workout, and then a cool down, with skill drills mixed in either after the warm up or before the cool down.

For example, when I was training for the Ironman, my coach had me perform "high knees" and "butt kickers" at the end of a training run. In high knees, I lifted my knees as high as possible while running for about fifty meters, then I walked back fifty meters and repeated this cycle six to eight times. In butt kickers, the motion is reversed so that during the running stride, I brought my heels up high, touching my buttocks as I ran. A cycle of butt kickers would also be repeated six to eight times.

Skill drill moves like these exaggerate the motions required during actual performance as a way to build both mental and physical muscle memory of the mechanical motion so that the proper form and movement become unconscious during actual competition.

Writers can use drills in the same way to the same effect. For writing drills, you take a specific component of the writing process—such as description, setting, characterization, dialogue, etcetera—and perform writing exercises devoted to those particular components. The result, or the intended outcome, is to build the creative "muscle memory" for those skills that will make them unconscious during the normal writing session and enhance overall writing performance.

By practicing specific skills and making mechanical movements unconscious, the athlete more easily enters into a flow state in which the physical exertion seems effortless. Similarly, by incorporating writing drills into your writing regimen, these skills become an unconscious part of your creative process, and entering a flow state in which the creative exertion seems effortless becomes much easier.

Two-a-Day Workouts

Some athletes train twice a day. In the morning, for example, an athlete may strength train with free weights or run wind sprints. Later in the day, after a period of recovery, she will perform another, different type of workout, such as a long, easy run. Splitting workouts into two-a-day can accelerate progress by allowing the athlete to do more in two workouts than would be possible with one longer workout. The key to this strategy is doing two different types of workout and allowing a period of recovery—at least several hours—between the efforts.

Writers can adapt this strategy to accelerate their progress on a book or other writing project. It is especially helpful for writers who are time constrained by other responsibilities. For example, you could do a fifteen to twenty minute high intensity writing workout in the morning, move on and attend to your other daily responsibilities, such as work or family obligations, and then return to the page in the evening for another writing session—this time a tempo session in which you type up or revise/rewrite what you wrote earlier, expanding as you go for about thirty to forty-five minutes. This two-a-day writing workout strategy amounts to one hour or less per day but could yield two to four pages of typescript draft material (depending on your flow and speed during each of the sessions).

This is a flexible strategy as well and can be adapted to fit virtually any daily schedule, including days when you have significant time constraints. Can you put together only ten minutes in the morning and ten minutes at night? That's fine. Can you only manage a single writing session most of the week and only do the two-a-day writing sessions once or twice a week, or even just occasionally? Then do that.

Remember, for endurance athletes, there are just a few basic principles and training strategies that apply to anyone, but these principles and strategies can be applied in myriad ways to suit the particular needs, schedules, goals, and preferences of each individual athlete. The same is true of writers—use these strategies by applying them in a way that suits your particular circumstances and needs on any given day—but use them. You will make progress.

The "Brick" Workout

A variation of the two-a-day workout is the brick workout, used by triathletes who, in competition, must quickly make the transition from one sport to another (swimming to biking to running, in that order) forcing their bodies to adapt to using tired muscles in a different way. In a brick workout, two different types of workouts are performed back-to-back, usually biking to running since both use primarily the leg muscles and these muscles must adapt to the different body mechanics involved in each discipline.

If you've never been involved in triathlons, imagine pushing the pedals of a bike for a few hours and then jumping off the bike and immediately starting to run—your feet and quadriceps would feel as if they are encased in cement. It's a physically (and mentally) difficult transition to make and that's why triathletes specifically train to make that transition easier using the brick workout. This type of workout enables the body to adapt to the specific demands of that quick transition, making it easier to accomplish during a competitive event.

The brick workout is another endurance training strategy that writers can adapt to condition the creative mind and it is simple to do. Most of the time when using the *ChiWriting* program, you will complete a single type of writing workout at a time. But as time allows, you can accelerate your progress and creative conditioning simply by performing back-to-back writing workouts. For example, you could complete an intense writing session for fifteen or twenty minutes, getting words on the page as quickly as possible without pause, and then immediately shift to a tempo writing workout.

If you've handwritten your high intensity writing session (my preferred method) you would immediately begin keyboarding what you wrote into typescript, typing quickly but expanding and refining a bit as you go, editing slightly, adding new thoughts, new notes to the work for about thirty to forty-five minutes. Accomplishing a brick workout trains your creative mind in a slightly different way compared to completing different types of writing workouts at different times or days throughout the week.

The brick workout is an excellent way to generate a good amount of draft material in a minimal amount of time (an hour or less using my example above) that will then get revised, rewritten, and expanded upon during long, slow distance writing workouts.

You could also use the brick workout as a "cross-training" strategy with writing and reading. For example, if you are writing a novel, you might start your brick workout by reading poetry, and then shifting directly to a writing workout in order to harness the energy and inspiration created by reading the poetry.

The Big Day

Remember that even though shorter high-intensity and tempo writing workouts are a good way to train your creative mind and generate a good amount of draft material to work with on the page in a relatively short amount of time, you will still need to perform the third type of workout: the long slow distance writing session — in order to further develop, refine, revise, and shape your material into a finished product.

An endurance athlete who uses shorter, more intense sessions to train still must actually run the full distance in competition and that means training on longer, slower runs, too, to ensure the physical and mental conditioning necessary to perform well over long distances. So in addition to shorter, more intense running workouts during the week, the athlete will also schedule a long slow distance run (say twelve or fifteen miles) at least once a week.

Over the course of your writing plan, you want to schedule in a long slow distance workout of at least two to three hours once or twice a week (typically on weekends or days you don't work) to build on the progress made during the shorter training sessions. Endurance athletes who focus on triathlon also sometimes use a training strategy called the "Big Day," in which they complete a long workout consisting of all three sports disciplines over the course of a multi-hour training day.

For example, a triathlete training for a full-distance Ironman triathlon (2.4-mile swim, 112-mile bike, and 26.2-mile run, in that order) will, at appropriate points during her training plan, schedule a Big Day in which she completes shorter versions of each triathlon leg. She may start in the morning with a long swim, transition to a long bike ride, and then finish with a long run. Depending on the athlete's speed and training volume, this might take anywhere from five to eight hours, or most of a day.

The Big Day is a valuable component of the triathlete's training program because it more closely resembles the time and effort of an actual event, which helps both physical and mental preparation. The triathlete who utilizes the Big Day strategy in training will be better prepared and perform better mentally and physically during the actual event.

The *ChiWriter* too can benefit from a Big Day strategy by incorporating into her training plan one day every six to eight weeks or so, or as often as her schedule and other responsibilities permit, in which a longer period of time—perhaps six to eight hours broken up by short breaks, if necessary—are devoted to working on her book.

For many writers who have other work and family responsibilities, this would likely mean a weekend day (or a day off from work). With the support of a partner or family members, the writer would clear her schedule of other responsibilities that day and focus on the book. The six to eight hours of a "Big Day" can be invested using all three types of writing workouts, or simply a single long slow distance writing workout to revise, rewrite, expand, and shape draft material already created during previous training sessions.

In the same way the Big Day strategy helps athletes prepare to complete an actual endurance event, the Big Day will also help you complete your project—utilizing and investing time wisely to make continual progress toward the goal: crossing the finish line of your book.

A FINAL WORD

"It is good to have an end to journey toward;
but it is the journey that matters in the end."
— Ursula K. LeGuin

When you devote months or years to the arduous process of achieving a difficult goal, there is an undeniable thrill when you reach the moment of fruition, that moment when the achievement becomes manifest.

I recall the excitement of being handed my MFA diploma after four years of hard work (two years to prepare and two years in the program) to achieve that goal. I recall the great sense of joy and relief I felt when I crossed the finish line of my Ironman race and a finisher medal was placed around my neck, completing many months of grueling preparation and training. Even as I write this, I feel a welling excitement within that I am nearing the finish line of this book.

My hope is that the ideas and strategies I've shared within these pages will help you to write your own book and that you will feel that same excitement and sense of accomplishment when you complete it.

Here are two things I've realized, though, that I'd like you to reflect upon as you prepare to employ these ideas and strategies:

- First, the feelings of excitement and joy when a goal is reached are directly proportional to the level of difficulty it took to reach it. *ChiWriting* gives you tools and strategies to develop a systematic process that makes completing your book possible, but that doesn't mean it's going to be easy. In fact, it likely will be difficult, especially in the beginning. Therefore, *embrace the difficulty*.

- Second, those feelings of excitement and joy — as sweet as they are — are fleeting. Once a goal is achieved, the rush of elation quickly subsides. But that's okay, because what is left in its place is far more enduring: feelings of greater confidence and deep pride in yourself. The feeling that you *can* accomplish anything you set your mind to, even if it seems impossible for you at the outset. When that happens, you realize that the most important thing is not that singular moment when you cross the finish line of a major goal, but the journey you took to get there. Therefore, *enjoy the journey*.

The ability to embrace the difficulty and enjoy the journey represent two more natural parallels between the world of the endurance athlete and the world of the writer — these two attributes are the greatest predictors of success in achieving your goal.

This book is ending, but yours is just beginning. You're on that rowboat in the middle of the ocean and on the distant horizon, among an infinite number of ports, is the one port you've made a commitment to reach.

The journey will be difficult.

Embrace the difficulty. Enjoy the journey.

ABOUT THE AUTHOR

T.A. (Tom) Pierce has been writing professionally for businesses since 1989. He received his MFA in Creative Writing from Spalding University and is a former USAT-certified Level I triathlon coach. *ChiWriting* is based on his experiences as a writer, MFA graduate, and triathlete, which includes training for and finishing a 140.6-mile Ironman race.

In addition to *ChiWriting*, he has completed a collection of short stories, some of which have appeared in respected journals such as *Quarterly West*, *American Literary Review*, and *Bellevue Literary Review*. He is also the recipient of an Emerging Artist award (in literary arts) from the Kentucky Arts Council. He lives in Louisville with his family and is currently at work on a novel.

Tom would love to hear about your experiences and results using the *ChiWriting* program and principles. Please email him at tom@chiwriting.com.

ACKNOWLEDGMENTS

I owe everlasting gratitude to a group of people so large I can't possibly name them all: the staff, faculty, students, and alumni of Spalding University's MFA program. It's hard to overstate the positive impact the program had on me. It continues to astound me that I actually had access to so many fine writers and creative minds, all of whom were incredibly generous with their time and talents, most especially my mentors Mary Yukari Waters, Mary Clyde, Kirby Gann, and K.L. Cook, but also Connie May Fowler, Crystal Wilkinson, Silas House, Neela Vaswani, Roy Hoffman, Robin Lippincott, Julie Brickman, and Phil Deaver.

The incredible long-time staff includes co-founder and program director Sena Jeter Naslund; co-founder and administrative director Karen Mann; associate program director Kathleen Driskell; and associate administrative director Katy Yocom. At the start of each residency, Sena always says "Welcome home" to all those gathered. Spalding *does* feel like home because Spalding MFA staff, faculty, students, and alumni feel like family.

I also wish to thank the staff, coaches, and teammates of the Leukemia and Lymphoma Society's Team in Training for introducing me to the sport of triathlon. It's hard to know whether triathlon actually saved my life or not, but for certain it immeasurably improved it. This book would not have been possible without the experience of endurance training and the insights it gave me into the creative process.

Thanks to Janet Wallace for her early encouragement. Janet was the first person I told about my nascent idea for *ChiWriting* and her immediate enthusiasm for the concept was inspiring (and also a little scary). Thanks also to my good friend Jessie Morgan, who helped me without even realizing it. Through regular talks with Jessie, I gained valuable insights that informed my thinking on portions of the book.

I owe special thanks to Terry Price. Once I fully committed to this project, I brought Terry on as my creative coach—the best decision I could have made. Terry is not only a talented writer and coach, he is one of the kindest, biggest-hearted people I know. His above-and-beyond support, guidance, and encouragement throughout the process—including creative and editorial insights into early drafts of each section—kept me accountable and moving forward. He is a friend and a light to many and I'm honored to know him.

I want to thank Anne Marie Fowler for her close reading of the complete manuscript and the valuable insights and editorial suggestions she offered. I also owe a second debt of gratitude to Kirby Gann for his editing expertise. Kirby is an extraordinary novelist and, thankfully, an incredibly smart editor, as well.

Finally, I am beyond grateful for my wife, Amy, always and in all ways.

APPENDIX:

SAMPLE SEASON AND WEEKLY TRAINING PLAN TEMPLATES

These templates are available as free downloads from www.chiwriting.com

ChiWriting

Sample Season Plan Template

Sample Weekly Writing Plan Template

NOTES

www.ingramcontent.com/pod-product-compliance
Lightning Source LLC
Chambersburg PA
CBHW051648040426
42446CB00009B/1040